John Mathew Gutch, John Hicklin

Robin Hood

A collection of poems, songs and ballads

John Mathew Gutch, John Hicklin

Robin Hood
A collection of poems, songs and ballads

ISBN/EAN: 9783744781626

Printed in Europe, USA, Canada, Australia, Japan

Cover: Foto ©Thomas Meinert / pixelio.de

More available books at **www.hansebooks.com**

ROBIN HOOD.

They Yorkshire woods frequented much,
   And Lancashire also :
Wherein their practises were such
   That they wrought mickle woe.

None rich durst travell to and fro,
   Though nere so strongly arm'd,
But by these theeves (so strong in show)
   They still were rob'd and harm'd.

His chiefest spight to th' clergie was,
   That liv'd in monstrous pride :
No one of them he would let passe
   Along the highway side.

But first they must to dinner go,
   And afterwards to shrift :
Full many a one he served so,
   Thus while he liv'd by theft.

No monks nor fryers would he let goe,
   Without paying their fees :
If they thought much to be us'd so,
   Their stones he made them leese.

For such as they the country fill'd
   With bastards in those dayes ;
Which to prevent, these sparkes did geld
   All that came by their ways.

But Robbin Hood so gentle was,
   And bore so brave a minde,
If any in distresse did passe,
   To them he was so kind :,

That he would give and lend to them,
   To helpe them in their neede ;
This made all poore men pray for him,
   And wish he well might speede.

The widdow and the fatherlesse
  He would send meanes unto ;
And those whom famine did oppresse
  Found him a friendly foe.

Nor would he doe a woman wrong,
  But see her safe conveid :
He would protect with power strong
  All those who crav'd his ayde.

The abbot of Saint Maries then,
  Who him undid before,
Was riding with two hundred men,
  And gold and silver store :

But Robbin Hood upon him set,
  With his couragious sparkes,
And all the coyne perforce did get,
  Which was twelve thousand markes.

He bound the abbot to a tree,
  And would not let him passe,
Before that to his men and he
  His lordship had said masse :

Which being done, upon his horse
  He set him fast astride,
And with his face towards his * * *
  He forced him to ride.

His men were faine to be his guide,
  For he rode backward home :
The abbot, being thus villified,
  Did sorely chafe and fume.

Thus Robin Hood did vindicate
  His former wrongs receiv'd :
For 'twas this covetous prelàte
  That him of land bereav'd.

The abbot he rode to the king,
 With all the haste he could;
And to his grace he every thing
 Exactly did unfold :

And sayd if that no course were ta'en,
 By force or stratagem,
To take this rebel and his traine,
 No man should passe for them.

The king protested by and by
 Unto the abbot then,
That Robbin Hood with speed should dye,
 With all his merry men.

But e're the king did any send,
 He did another feate,
Which did his grace much more offend,
 The fact indeed was great :

For in a short time after that
 The kings receivers went
Towards London with the coyne they got,
 For 's highness northerne rent :

Bold Robbin Hood and Little John,
 With the rest of their traine,
Not dreading law, set them upon,
 And did their gold obtaine.

The king much moved at the same,
 And the abbots talke also,
In this his anger did proclaime,
 And sent word to and fro,

That whosoe'er alive or dead
 Could bring bold Robbin Hood,
Should have one thousand markes well paid
 In gold and silver good.

H

This promise of the king did make
    Full many yeomen bold,
Attempt stout Robbin Hood to take
    With all the force they could.

But still when any came to him
    Within the gay greene wood,
He entertainement gave to them
    With venison fat and good ;

And shew'd to them such martiale sport
    With his long bow and arrow,
That they of him did give report,
    How that it was great sorrow,

That such a worthy man as he
    Should thus be put to shift,
Being late a lord of high degree,
    Of living quite bereft.

The king to take him, more and more,
    Sent men of mickle might ;
But he and his still beate them sore,
    And conquered them in fight :

Or else with love and courtesie,
    To him he won their hearts.
Thus still he lived by robbery
    Throughout the northerne parts ;

And all the country stood in dread
    Of Robbin Hood and 's men :
For stouter lads ne're liv'd by bread
    In those days, nor since then.

The abbot which before I nam'd,
    Sought all the meanes he could
To have by force this rebele ta'ne,
    And his adherents bold.

Therefore he arm'd five hundred men,
  With furniture compleate ;
But the outlawes slew halfe of them,
  And made the rest retreate.

The long bow and the arrow keene
  They were so us'd unto,
That still he kept the forrest greene
  In spight o' th' proudest foe.

Twelve of the abbots men he tooke,
  Who came him to have ta'ne,
When all the rest the field forsooke,
  These he did entertaine :

With banquetting and merriment,
  And, having us'd them well,
He to their lord them safely sent,
  And will'd them him to tell,

That if he would be pleas'd at last
  To beg of our good king,
That he might pardon what was past,
  And him to favour bring,

He would surrender backe again
  The money which before
Was taken by him and his men
  From him and many more.

Poore men might safely passe by him,
  And some that way would chuse,
For well they knew that to helpe them
  He evermore did use.

But where he knew a mizer rich
  That did the poore oppresse,
To feel his coyne his hands did itch,
  He'd have it more or lesse :

And sometimes, when the high-way fayl'd,
   Then he his courage rouses,
He and his men have oft assayld
   Such rich men in their houses.

So that, through dread of Robbin then,
   And his adventurous crew,
The mizers kept great store of men,
   Which else maintayn'd but few.

King Richard, of that name the first,
   Sirnamed Cuer de Lyon,
Went to defeate the Pagans curst,
   Who kept the coasts of Syon.

The bishop of Ely chancelor,
   Was left a vice-roy here,
Who, like a potent emperor,
   Did proudly domminere

Our chronicles of him report,
   That commonly he rode
With a thousand horse from court to court,
   Where he would make abode.

He, riding down towards the north,
   With his aforesayd train,
Robbin and his men did issue forth,
   Them all to entertaine ;

And with the gallant gray-goose wing
   They shewd to them such playe,
That made their horses kicke and fling,
   And downe their riders lay.

Full glad and faine the bishop was,
   For all his thousand men,
To seek what meanes he could to passe
   From out of Robbins ken.

Two hundred of his men were kil'd,
  And fourescore horses good,
Thirty, who did as captives yeeld,
  Were carryed to the greene wood ;

Which afterwards were ransomed,
  For twenty markes a man :
The rest set spurres to horse, and fled
  To th' town of Warrington.

The bishop sore enraged then,
  Did, in king Richards name,
Muster a power of northerne men,
  These outlawes bold to tame.

But Robbin with his courtesie
  So wonne the meaner sort,
That they were loath on him to try
  What rigor did import.

So that bold Robbin and his traine
  Did live unhurt of them,
Untill king Richard came againe
  From faire Jerusalem :

And then the talke of Robbin Hood
  His royal eares did fill ;
His grace admir'd that i' th' greene wood
  He thus continued still.

So that the country farre and neare
  Did give him great applause ;
For none of them neede stand in feare,
  But such as broke the lawes.

He wished well unto the king,
  And prayed still for his health,
And never practis'd any thing
  Against the common-wealth.

Onely, because he was undone
　By th' crewele clergie then ;
All meanes that he could thinke upon
　To vexe such kinde of men,

He enterpriz'd with hateful spleene ;
　For which he was to blame,
For fault of some to wreake his teene
　On all that by him came.

With wealth which he by robbery got
　Eight almes-houses he built,
Thinking thereby to purge the blot
　Of blood which he had spilt.

Such was their blinde devotion then,
　Depending on their workes ;
Which if 'twere true, we Christian men
　Inferiour were to Turkes.

But, to speak true of Robbin Hood,
　And wrong him not a jot,
He never would shed any mans blood
　That him invaded not.

Nor would he injure husbandmen,
　That toyld at cart and plough ;
For well he knew, were't not for them
　To live no man knew how.

The king in person, with some lords,
　To Nottingham did ride,
To try what strength and skill affords
　To crush these outlaws pride.

And, as he once before had done,
　He did againe proclaime,
That whosoe'er would take upon
　To bring to Nottingham,

Or any place within the land,
    Rebellious Robbin Hood,
Should be prefer'd in place to stand
    With those of noble blood.

When Robbin Hood heard of the same,
    Within a little space,
Into the towne of Nottingham
    A letter to his grace

He shot upon an arrow head,
    One evening cunningly ;
Which was brought to the king, and read
    Before his majestie.

The tennure of this letter was
    That Robbin would submit,
And be true liegeman to his grace
    In any thing that's fit,

So that his highnesse would forgive
    Him and his merry men all ;
If not, he must i' th' green wood live,
    And take what chance did fall.

The king would faine have pardoned him,
    But that some lords did say,
This president will much condemn
    Your grace another day.

While that the king and lords did stay
    Debating on this thing,
Some of these outlawes fled away
    Unto the Scottish king.

For they suppos'd, if he were tane
    Or to the king did yeeld,
By th' commons all the rest of 's train
    Full quickely would be quell'd.

Of more than full an hundred men,
    But forty tarryed still,
Who were resolv'd to sticke to him
    Let fortune worke her will.

If none had fled, all for his sake
    Had got their pardon free ;
The king to favour meant to take
    His merry men and he.

But e're the pardon to him came
    This famous archer dy'd :
His death and manner of the same
    I'le presently describe.

For, being vext to think upon
    His followers revolt,
In melancholly passion
    He did recount his fault.

Perfideous traytors ! sayd he then,
    In all your dangers past
Have I you guarded as my men,
    To leave me thus at last !

This sad perplexity did cause
    A feaver, as some say,
Which him unto confusion drawes,
    Though by a stranger way.

This deadly danger to prevent,
    He hie'd him with all speede
Unto a nunnery, with intent
    For his healths-sake to bleede.

A faithlesse fryer did pretend
    In love to let him blood,
But he by falshood wrought the end
    Of famous Robbin Hood.

The fryer, as some say, did this
    To vindicate the wrong :
Which to the clergy he and his
    Had done by power strong.

Thus dyed he by trechery,
    That could not dye by force :
Had he liv'd longer, certainely
    King Richard, in remorse,

Had unto favour him receiv'd,
    ' His ' brave men elevated :
'Tis pitty he was of life bereav'd
    By one which he so hated.

A treacherous leach this fryer was,
    To let him bleed to death ;
And Robbin was, methinks, an asse
    To trust him with his breath.

His corpse the prioress of the place,
    The next day that he dy'd,
Caused to be buried, in mean case,
    Close by the high-way side.

And over him she caused a stone
    To be fixed on the ground,
An epitaph was set thereon,
    Wherein his name was found ;

The date o' th' yeare and day also,
    Shee made to be set there ;
That all, who by the way did goe,
    Might see it plain appeare,

That such a man as Robbin Hood
    Was buried in that place ;
And how he lived in the greene wood
    And robb'd there for a space.

It seemes that though the clergie he
  Had put to mickle woe,
He should not quite forgotten be,
  Although he was their foe.

This woman, though she did him hate,
  Yet loved his memory ;
And thought it wondrous pitty that
  His fame should with him dye.

This epitaph, as records tell,
  Within this hundred yeares,
By many was discerned well,
  But time all things out-weares.

His followers, when he was dead,
  Were some receiv'd to grace ;
The rest to forraign countries fled,
  And left their native place.

Although his funerall was but mean,
  This woman had in minde,
Least his fame should be buried clean
  From those that came behind.

For certainly, before nor since,
  No man e're understood,
Under the reigne of any prince,
  Of one like Robbin Hood.

Full thirteene years, and something more,
  These outlawes lived thus ;
Feared of the rich, loved of the poor :
  A thing most marvelous.

A thing unpossible to us
  This story seems to be ;
None dares be now so venturous,
  But times are chang'd we see.

We that live in these later dayes
    Of civile government,
If need be, have an hundred wayes
    Such outlawes to prevent.

In those dayes men more barbarous were,
    And lived lesse in awe ;
Now (god be thanked) people feare
    More to offend the law.

No roaring guns were then in use,
    They dreampt of no such thing ;
Our Englishmen in fight did chuse
    The gallant gray-goose wing :

In which activity these men,
    Through practise, were so good,
That in those days none equal'd them,   .
    Specially Robbin Hood.

So that, it seemes, keeping in caves,
    In woods and forests thicke,
They'd beate a multitude with staves,
    Their arrowes did so pricke :

And none durst neare unto them come,
    Unlesse in courtesie ;
All such he bravely would send home
    With mirth and jollity :

Which courtesie won him such love,
    As I before have told,
'Twas the cheef cause that he did prove
    More prosperous than he could.

Let us be thankefull for these times
    Of plenty, truth and peace ;
And leave out great and horrid crimes,
    Least they cause this to cease.

I know there's many fained tales
  Of Robbin Hood and 's crew ;
But chronicles, which seldome fayles,
  Reports this to be true.

Let none then thinke this is a lye,
  For, if 'twere put to th' worst,
They may the truth of all discry
  I' th' raigne of Richard the first.

If any reader please to try,
  As I direction show,
The truth of this brave history,
  Hee'll find it true I know.

And I shall thinke my labour well
  Bestowed to purpose good,
When't shall be said that I did tell
  True tales of Robbin Hood.

ROBIN HOOD'S BIRTH, BREEDING, VALOUR, AND MARRIAGE.

This Ballad is from a black-letter copy in the Collection formerly belonging to Thomas Pearson, Esq. but now in the British Museum. Its original title is "A new ballad of bold Robin Hood, shewing his birth, breeding, valour, and marriage at Titbury (Tutbury) Bull-running. Calculated for the meridian of Staffordshire, but may serve for Derbyshire or Kent." Printed in 1670.

Tutbury is a town in Staffordshire, famous for the ruins of an ancient castle on a commanding eminence, and also for its sport of bull-baiting in the olden time.

KIND gentlemen, will you be patient awhile?
    Ay, and then you shall hear anon
A very good ballad of bold Robin Hood,
    And of his man brave Little John.*

In Locksly town, in merry Nottinghamshire,
    In merry sweet Locksly town,
There bold Robin Hood he was born and was bred,
    Bold Robin of famous renown.

The father of Robin a forrester was,
    And he shot in a lusty strong bow
Two north country miles and an inch at a shot,
    As the Pinder of Wakefield does know.

* Little John. "Little John, cujus coxendia, in Scotia asservatus, quatuordecim pedum altitudinem habuisse dicitur." *Johnson's Thaumatographia*, p. 456.—Note in *Mr. Douce's* handwriting.

For he brought Adam Bell, and Clim of the Clugh,
   And William of "Clowdesle,"
To shoot with our forrester for forty mark,
   And the forrester beat them all three.

His mother was neece to the Coventry knight,
   Which Warwickshire men call sir Guy ;*
For he slew the blue bore that hangs up at the
     gate,
   Or mine host of the Bull tells a lie.

Her brother was Gamwel, of Great Gamwel-Hal,†
   A noble house-keeper was he,
Ay, as ever broke bread in sweet Nottingham-
     shire,
   And a 'squire of famous degree.

The mother of Robin said to her husbànd,
   My honey; my love, and my dear,
Let Robin and I ride this morning to Gamwel,
   · To taste of my brother's good cheer.

And he said, I grant thee thy boon, gentle Joan,
   Take one of my horses, I pray :
The sun is arising, and therefore make haste,
   For to-morrow is Christmas-day.

* Guy Earl of Warwick.—Note by *Stukeley.*

† "George Gamwell, of Gamwell Hall *magna,* Esq.
Joanna, wife of Fitz Odoth, had issue Robin Fitz Odoth.
Gamwell, the king's forester in Yorkshire, mentioned in
Camden. See my answer, No. 11 of Lady Roisia, where
is Robin Hood's true pedigree."—*Stukeley.*
   "Dr. Stukeley here refers to No. 2 of his *Palæographia
Britannica,* p. 115."—*Douce.* "See also Lamb's notes to
the battle of Flodden field, p. 80. Pegge and Dr. Percy
were of opinion he was so named, *quasi* Robbing Hode,
and by vulgar fiction only Earl of Huntington. See Mr.
Gough's remarks on this subject in *Gent's Mag.* 1793,
p. 225."—*Douce.*

Then Robin Hood's father's grey gelding was
    brought,
  And sadled and bridled was he ;
God-wot a blue bonnet, his new suit of cloaths
  And a cloak that did reach to his knee.

She got on her hoiyday kirtle and gown,
  They were of a light Lincoln green ;
The cloath was homespun, but for colour and
    make
  It might 'have beseemed' our queen.

And then Robin got on his basket-hilt sword,
  And his dagger on his tother side ;
And said, my dear mother, let's haste to be gone,
  We have forty long miles to ride.

When Robin had mounted his gelding so grey,
  His father, without any trouble,
Set her up behind him, and bad her not fear,
  For his gelding had oft carried double.

And when she was settled, they rode to their
    neighbours,
  And drank and shook hands with them all ;
And then Robin gallopt, and never gave o're,
  'Till they lighted at Gamwel-Hall.

And now you may think the right worshipful
    'squire
  Was joyful his sister to see ;
For he kist her, and kist her, and swore a great
    oath,
  Thou art welcome, kind sister, to me.

To-morrow, when mass had been said in the
    chappel,
  Six tables were covered in the hall,

And in comes the 'squire, and makes a short
    speech,
  It was, Neighbours, you're welcome all.

But not a man here shall taste my March beer,
  'Till a Christmas carrol he sing.
Then all clapt their hands, and they shouted and
    sung,
  'Till the hall and the parlour did ring.

Now mustard and brawn, roast beef and plumb
    pies,
  Were set upon every table :
And noble George Gamwel said, eat and be merry,
  And drink too as long as you're able.

When dinner was ended, his chaplain said grace,
  And, be merry, my friends, said the 'squire ;
It rains, and it blows, but call for more ale,
  And lay some more wood on the fire.

And now call ye Little John hither to me,
  For Little John is a fine lad,
At gambols and juggling, and twenty such tricks,
  As shall make you both merry and glad.

When Little John came, to gambols they went,
  Both gentlemen, yeomen, and clown ;
And what do you think ? Why, as true as I
    live,
  Bold Robin Hood put them all down.

And now you may think the right worshipful
    'squire
  Was joyful this sight for to see ;
For he said, Cousin Robin, thou'st go no more
    home,
  But tarry and dwell here with me :

Thou shalt have my land when I die, and till then,
Thou shalt be the staff of my age.
Then grant me my boon, dear uncle, said Robin,
That Little John may be my page.

And he said, kind cousin, I grant thee thy boon ;
With all my heart, so let it be.
Then come hither, Little John, said Robin Hood,
Come hither my page unto me :

Go fetch me my bow, my longest long bow,
And broad arrows, one, two, or three.
For when 'tis fair weather we'll into Sherwood,
Some merry pastime to see.

When Robin Hood came into merry Sherwood,
He winded his bugle so clear ;
And twice five and twenty good yeomen and bold,
Before Robin Hood did appear.

Where are your companions all ? said Rob Hood,
For still I want forty and three.
Then said a bold yeoman, Lo, yonder they stand,
All under a green wood tree.

As that word was spoke, Clorinda came by,
The queen of the shepherds was she ;
And her gown was of velvet as green as the grass,
And her buskin did reach to her knee.

Her gait it was graceful, her body was straight,
And her countenance free from pride ;
A bow in her hand, and quiver and arrows
Hung dangling by her sweet side.

Her eye-brows were black, ay, and so was her hair,
And her skin was as smooth as glass ;
Her visage spoke wisdom, and modesty too :
Sets with Robin Hood such a lass !

I

Said Robin Hood, Lady fair, whither away
O whither, fair lady, away ?
And she made him an answer, to kill a fat buck ;
For to-morrow is Titbury day.

Said Robin Hood, Lady fair, wander with me
A little to yonder green bower ;
There set down to rest you, and you shall be sure
Of a brace or a 'leash' in an hour.

And as we were going towàrds the green bower,
Two hundred good bucks we espy'd ;
She chose out the fattest that was in the herd,
And she shot him through side and side.

By the faith of my body, said bold Robin Hood,
I never saw woman like thee ;
And com'st thou from east, or com'st thou from
west,
Thou need'st not beg venison of me.

However, along to my bower you shall go,
And taste of a forrester's meat :
And when we came thither we found as good cheer
As any man needs for to eat.

For there was hot venison, and warden pies* cold,
Cream clouted, with honey-combs plenty ;
And the sarvitors they were beside Little John,
Good yeomen at least four and twenty.

Clorinda said, tell me your name, gentle sir ;
And he said, 'tis bold Robin Hood :
'Squire Gamwel's my uncle, but all my delight
Is to dwell in the merry Sherwood ;

* *Wardens* are a species of large pears. In Shakspere's
"Winter's Tale," the clown, enumerating the articles he
had to provide for the sheep-shearing feast, says he "must
have saffron to colour the *warden pies*."

For 'tis a fine life, and 'tis void of all strife.
  So 'tis, sir, Clorinda reply'd.
But oh ! said bold Robin, how sweet would it be,
  If Clorinda would be my bride !

She blusht at the motion ; yet, after a pause
  Said, Yes, sir, and with all my heart.
Then let us send for a priest, said Robin Hood,
  And be married before we do part.

But she said, it may not be so, gentle sir,
  For I must be at Titbury feast ;
And if Robin Hood will go thither with me,
  I'll make him the most welcome guest.

Said Robin Hood, reach me that buck, Little
    John,
  For I'll go along with my dear ;
And bid my yeomen kill six brace of bucks,
  And meet me to-morrow just here.

Before he had ridden five Staffordshire miles,
  Eight yeomen, that were too bold,
Bid Robin Hood stand, and deliver his buck;
  A truer tale never was told.

I will not, faith, said bold Robin ; come, John,
  Stand by me, and we'll beat 'em all.
Then both drew their swords, and so cut 'em and
    slasht 'em,
  That five of them did fall.

The three that remain'd call'd to Robin for
    quarter,
  And pitiful John begg'd their lives :
When John's boon was granted, he gave them
    good counsel,
  And sent them all home to their wives.

This battle was fought near to Titbury town,*
  When the bagpipers baited the bull ;
I'm the king of the fidlers, and I swear 'tis truth,
  And I call him that doubts it a gull :

* Tutbury, or Stutesbury, Staffordshire. This celebrated
place lies about four miles from Burton-upon-Trent, on
the west bank of the river Don.   Its castle, it is supposed,
was built a considerable time before the Norman conquest.
Being the principal seat of the Dukes of Lancaster, it was
long distinguished as the scene of festivity and splendour.
The number of minstrels, which crowded it, was so great,
that it was found necessary to have recourse to some ex-
pedient for preserving order among them, and determining
their claims of precedence.   Accordingly one of their
number, with the title of king of the minstrels, was appointed, and under him several inferior officers to assist
in the execution of the laws.   To this chief a charter was
granted, by John of Gaunt, Duke of Lancaster, 22nd
August, 4th Richard II. 1381.   This king of the minstrels
and his officers having inflicted fines and punishments,
which exceeded the due bounds of justice, a court for
hearing and determining complaints and controversies was
instituted, which was yearly held with many forms and
ceremonies.   The business of the court being concluded,
the officers withdraw to partake of a sumptuous repast,
prepared for them by the steward of the lordship.   In
the afternoon the minstrels assembled at the gate of the
priory, where by way of amusement for the multitude, a
bull, having his horns, ears, and tail cut off, his body
besmeared with soap, and his nose blown full of pepper,
was then let loose.   If the minstrels could take and hold
him, even so long as to deprive him of the smallest portion
of his hair, he was declared their property, provided this
was done within the confines of Staffordshire, and before
sunset.   The bull was next collared and roped, and being
brought to the market cross was baited with dogs.   After
this he was delivered to the minstrels, who might dispose
of him as they deemed proper.
  An Inspeximus by Henry VI. relative to the customs of
Tutbury, makes mention of this extraordinary one in the
following words:—"There is an ancient practice belonging
to the honor of Tutbury, that the minstrels who com

For I saw them fighting, and fiddled the while,
  And Clorinda sung "Hey derry down!
The bumkins are beaten, put up thy sword, Bob,
  And now let's dance into the town.

Before we came to it, we heard a strange shouting,
  And all that were in look'd madly;
For some were on bull-back, some dancing a
    morris,
  And some singing *Arthur-a-Bradly.*

And there we see Thomas, our justices clerk,
  And Mary, to whom he was kind;
For Tom rode before her, and call'd Mary madam,
  And kiss'd her full sweetly behind:

And so may your worships. But we went to
    dinner,
  With Thomas and Mary, and Nan;
They all drank a health to Clorinda, and told her,
  Bold Robin Hood was a fine man.

When dinner was ended, sir Roger, the parson
  Of Dubbridge, was sent for in haste:

to matins there, on the feast of the Assumption of the
Blessed Virgin, shall have a bull given by the prior of
Tutbury, if they can take him on this side of the river
Don, which is next to Tutbury; or else the prior shall
give them xld.; for the enjoyment of which custom they
shall give to the lord, at the said feast, yearly xxd."

In consequence of the outrages committed at this bull-
running and baiting, an end was put to the barbarous
custom, by commutation, between seventy and eighty
years since. An annual court, however, called the Minstrels' Court, continued to be held at the steward's house,
which was situated on a part of the site of the ancient
castle. The Duke of Devonshire is the owner of the
priory. *Vide* "Blount's Ancient Tenures," "Hawkins's
History of Music," "Strutt's Sports and Pastimes," for
fuller particulars of this ancient custom.

He brought his mass-book, and he bad them
    take hands,
  And joyn'd them in marriage full fast.

And then, as bold Robin Hood and his sweet bride
  Went hand in hand to the green bower,
The birds sung with pleasure in merry Sherwood,
  And 'twas a most joyful hour.

And when Robin came in sight of the bower,
  Where are my yeomen ? said he :
And Little John answer'd, lo, yonder they stand,
  All under the green wood tree.

Then a garland they brought her by two and
    by two,
  And plac'd them at the bride's bed :
The music struck up, and we all fell to dance,
  'Till the bride and the bridegroom were a-bed.

And what they did there must be counsel to me,
  Because they lay long the next day ;
And I had haste home, but I got a good piece
  Of bride-cake, and so came away.

Now out, alas ! I had forgotten to tell ye,
  That marry'd they were with a ring ;
And so will Nan Knight, or be buried a maiden,
  And now let us pray for the king :.

That he may get children, and they may get more,
  To govern and do us some good :
And then I'll make ballads in Robin Hood's
    bower,
  And sing 'em in merry Sherwood.

Nottingham in 1680.—P. 119.

ROBIN HOOD'S PROGRESS TO NOTTINGHAM.

From an old black-letter copy in the Collection of Anthony
à Wood. It is there said to go "To the tune of Bold Robin
Hood;" and the chorus is repeated in every stanza. To
the above title are added the following doggerel lines:

> Where hee met with fifteen forresters all on a row,
> And hee desired of them some news for to know,
> But with crosse grain'd words they did him thwart,
> For which at last hee made them smart.*

Robin Hood he was a tall young man,
          Derry, derry down,
  And fifteen winters old ;
And Robin Hood he was a proper young man,
  Of courage stout and bold.
          Hey down, derry, derry down.
Robin Hood he would unto fair Nottingham,
  With the general for to dine ;
There was hee ware of fifteen forresters,
  And a drinking bear, ale, and wine.†

---

* There are two copies of this ballad in the Roxburgh
Collection, now placed on the shelves of the British
Museum, with which this has been collated and a few
corrections made.
† The following stanza is extracted from a note in Mr.
Douce's hand-writing in his copy of Ritson's edition of
"Robin Hood" bequeathed by Mr. D. to the Bodleian
Library, and which formerly belonged to Dr. Stukeley,

What news? What news? said bold Robin Hood,
    What news fain wouldest thou know?
Our king hath provided a shooting match,
    And I'm ready with my bow.

We hold it in scorn then, said the forrestèrs,
    That ever a boy so young
Should bear a bow before our king,
    That's not able to draw one string.

I'le hold you twenty marks, said bold Robin Hood,
    By the leave of our lady,
That I'le hit a mark a hundred rod,*
    And I'le cause a hart to dye.

We'l hold you twenty mark, then said the forrestèrs,
    By the leave of our lady,
Thou hit'st not the marke a hundred rod,
    Nor causest a hart to dye.

Robin Hood he bent up a noble bow,
    And a broad arrow he let flye,
He hit the mark a hundred rod,
    And he caused a hart to dye.

Some said he brake ribs one or two,
    And some say hee brake three;

having his autograph in the title-page, as well as some
notes in the doctor's writing:
    When Robin came to Nottingham,
        Derry, derry, down,
      His dinner all for to dine;
    There met him fifteen jolly foresters,
      Were drinking ale and wine.
    [DUKE OF NEWCASTLE's play of *The Varietie*, p. 57.

* Poles, perches. A rod, pole, or perch, is usually sixteen feet and a half, but in Sherwood forest (according to
Blount) it is twenty-one feet, the foot there being eighteen
inches.

The arrow in the hart would not abide,
  But it glanced in two or three.

The hart did skip, and the hart did leap,
  And the hart lay on the ground ;
The wager is mine, said bold Robin Hood,
  If't were for a thousand pound.

The wager's none of thine, then said the forrestèrs,
  Although thou beest in haste ;
Take up thy bow, and get thee hence,
  Lest wee thy sides do baste.

Robin Hood he took up his noble bow,
  And his broad arrows all amain ;
And Robin Hood he laught, and begun to smile,
  As he went over the plain.

Then Robin hee bent his noble bow,
  And his broad arrowes he let flye,
Till fourteen of these fifteen forrestèrs
  Upon the ground did lye.

He that did this quarrel first begin,
  Went tripping over the plain ;
But Robin Hood he bent his noble bow,
  And hee fecht him back again.

You said I was no archer, said Robin Hood,
  But say so now again ;
With that he sent another arròw,
  That split his head in twain.

You have found mee an archer, said Robin Hood,
  Which will make your wives for to wring,
And wish that you had never spoke the word,
  That I could not draw one string.

The people that lived in fair Nottinghàm
　　Came running out amain,
Supposing to have taken bold Robin Hood,
　　With the forresters that were slain.

Some lost legs, and some lost arms,
　　And some did lose their blood ;
But Robin hee took up his noble bow,
　　And is gone to the merry green wood.

They carried these forresters into fair Nottingham,
　　As many there did know ;
They dig'd them graves in their church-yard,
　　And they burried them all on a row.*

* A few days ago as some labourers were digging in a garden at Fox-lane, near Nottingham, they discovered six human skeletons entire, deposited in regular order side by side, supposed to be part of the fifteen foresters that were killed by Robin Hood. Near the above place anciently stood a church, built in the early ages of christianity, dedicated to St. Michael, which was totally demolished at the Reformation. Yet still the parishioners, on certain times repair to this place for religious purposes, it being considered as consecrated ground. In this place at different times great quantities of human bones have been found, besides several Saxon and old English coins, &c. &c.—*Gentleman's Magazine, April*, 1796. A similar discovery of human remains was also made in this locality during the year 1864, when excavating the ground for the foundations of new houses.

ROBIN HOOD AND THE STRANGER.

FROM an old black-letter copy in the Collection of Anthony
à Wood. The title now given to this ballad is that which
it seems to have originally borne; having been foolishly
altered to "Robin Hood newly revived." The circum-
stances attending the second part will be explained in a
note.—*Ritson.*

Corrected with the copy which was Major Pearson's,
now in the British Museum.—*Editor.*

COME listen awhile, you gentlemen all,
　　　With a hey down, down, a down, down,
　That are this bower within,
For a story of gallant bold Robin Hood,
　I purpose now to begin.

What time of day? quoth Robin Hood then;
　Quoth Little John, 'tis in the prime.
Why then we will to the green wood gang,
　For we have no vittles to dine.

As Robin Hood walkt the forrest along,
　It was in the mid of the day,
There he was met of a deft* young man,
　As ever walkt on the way.

His doublet was of silk, he said,
　His stockings like scarlet shone;
As he walked on along the way,
　To Robin Hood then unknown.

* Well-looking, neatly drest.

A herd of deer was in the bend,
  All feeding before his face :
Now the best of you ile have to my dinnèr,
  And that in a little space.

Now the stranger he made no mickle adoe,
  But he bends a right good bow,
And the best buck in the herd he slew,
  Forty good yards him froe.

Well shot, well shot, quod Robin Hood then,
  That shot it was shot in time ;
And if thou wilt accept of the place,
  Thou shalt be a bold yeoman of mine.

Go play the chiven,* the stranger said,
  Make haste and quickly go,
Or with my fist, be sure of this,
  Ile give thee buffets sto'.

Thou had'st not best buffet me, quod Robin Hood,
  For though I seem forlorn,
Yet I can have those that will take my part,
  If I but blow my horn.

Thou wast not best wind thy horn, the stranger
      said,
  Beest thou never so much in haste,
For I can draw out a good broad sword,
  And quickly cut the blast.

Then Robin Hood bent a very good bow
  To shoot, and that he would fain ;

---

  * Mr. Ritson queries this word without remark. We can
only offer a bare conjecture as to its meaning. Shiver was
anciently written *chiver*, of which there are examples in
Chaucer and Gower, and it is possible that *chiven* is a
derivative, signifying *coward* or *trembler*, but we can pro-
duce no authority in support of thi interpretation.—Ed.

The stranger he bent a very good bow,
  To shoot at bold Robin again.
O hold thy hand, hold thy hand, quod Robin
    Hood,
  To shoot it would be in vain ;
For if we should shoot the one at the other,
  The one of us may be slain.

But let's take our swords and our broad bucklèrs,
  And gang under yonder tree.
As I hope to be sav'd, the stranger said,
  One foot I will not flee.

Then Robin Hood lent the stranger a blow,
  'Most scar'd him out of his wit :
Thou never felt blow, the stranger he said,
  That shall be better quit.

The stranger he drew out a good broad sword,
  And hit Robin on the crown,
That from every haire of bold Robin's head
  The blood ran trickling down.

God a mercy,* good fellow ! quod Robin Hood,
    then,
  And for this that thou hast done,
Tell me, good fellow, what thou art,
  Tell me where thou doest wone.†

The stranger then answer'd bold Robin Hood,
  Ile tell thee where I did dwell ;
In Maxwell‡ town I was bred and born,
  My name is young Gamwel.

For killing of my own father's stewàrd,
  I am forc'd to this English wood,

* Gramercy, thanks. *Grand merci,* Fr.
† Dwell.—*Chaucer.*   ‡ Maxfield, in one edition

And for to seek an uncle of mine,
  Some call him Robin Hood.

But art thou a cousin of Robin Hood then?
  The sooner we should have done.
As I hope to be sav'd, the stranger then said,
  I am his own sister's son.

But, lord! what kissing and courting was there,
  When these two cousins did greet!
And they went all that summer's day,
  And Little John did [not] meet.

But when they met with Little John,
  He unto them did say,
O master, pray where have you been,
  You have tarried so long away?

I met with a stranger, quod Robin Hood,
  Full sore he hath beaten me.
Then I'le have a bout with him, quod Little John,
  And try if he can beat me.

Oh no, oh no, quoth Robin Hood then,
  Little John, it may not be so;
For he is my own dear sister's son,
  And cousins I have no mo.

But he shall be a bold yeoman of mine,
  My chief man next to thee;
And I Robin Hood, and thou Little John,
  And Scalock* he shall be.

And we'll be three of the bravest outlàws
  That live in the north country.
If you will hear more of bold Robin Hood,
  · In the second part it will be.

---

* The Roxburgh edition reads Scarlet; elsewhere, Scadlock.

[PART THE SECOND.*]

Now Robin Hood, Will Scadlock, and Little John
   Are walking over the plain,
With a good fat buck, which Will Scadlòck,
   With his strong bow had slain.

* This (from an old black-letter copy in Major Pearson's
collection) is evidently the genuine second part of the present ballad : though constantly printed as an independent
article, under the title of "Robin Hood, Will Scadlock,
and Little John : Or, a narrative of their victories obtained
against the prince of Aragon and the two giants ; and how
Will Scadlock married the princess. Tune of Robin Hood :
or Hey down, down, a down :" Instead of which, in all
former editions, are given the following incoherent stanzas,
which have all the appearance of being the fragment of a
different ballad :—*Ritson.*

THEN bold Robin Hood to the north he would go,
   With valour and mickle might,
With sword by his side, which oft had been tri'd,
   To fight and recover his right.

The first that he met was a bonny bold Scot,
   His servant he said he would be.
No, quoth Robin Hood, it cannot be good,
   For thou wilt prove false unto me :

Thou hast not been true to sire nor cuz.
   Nay, marry, the Scot, he said,
As true as your heart, I'le never part,
   Gude master, be not afraid.

Then Robin turned his face to the east,
   Fight on, my merry men stout ;
Our cause is good, quod brave Robin Hood,
   And we shall not be beaten out.

The battel grows hot on every side,
   The Scotchman made great moan :
Quoth Jockey, gude faith, they fight on each side,
   Would I were with my wife Joan !

Jog on, jog on, cries Robin Hood,
    The day it runs full fast;
For tho' my nephew me a breakfast gave,
    I have not yet broke my fast.

Then to yonder lodge let us take our way,
    I think it wondrous good,
Where my nephew by my bold yeomèn
    Shall be welcom'd unto the green-wood.

With that he took his bugle-horn,
    Full well he could it blow;
Streight from the woods came marching down
    One hundred tall fellows and mo.

Stand, stand to your arms, crys Will Scadlòck,
    Lo! the enemies are within ken.
With that Robin Hood he laugh'd aloud,
    Crying, they are my bold yeomèn.

Who, when they arriv'd, and Robin espy'd,
    Cry'd, master, what is your will?
We thought you had in danger been,
    Your horn did sound so shrill.

Now nay, now nay, quoth Robin Hood,
    The danger is past and gone;
I would have you welcome my nephew here,
    That has paid me two for one.

The enemy compast brave Robin about,
    'Tis long ere the battel ends;
Ther's neither will yield, nor give up the field,
    For both are supplied with friends.

This song it was made in Robin Hood's dayes:
    Let's pray unto Jove above,
To give us true peace, that mischief may cease,
    And war may give place unto love.

In feasting and sporting they pass'd the day,
   Till Phœbus sunk into the deep ;
Then each one to his quarters hy'd,
   His guard there for to keep.

Long had they not walk'd within the green-wood,
   But Robin he soon espy'd,
A beautiful damsel all alone,
   That on a black palfrey did ride.

Her riding-suit was of a sable hue black,
   Cypress over her face,
Through which her rose-like cheeks did blush,
   All with a comely grace.

Come tell me the cause, thou pretty one,
   Quoth Robin, and tell me aright,
From whence thou comest, and whither thou goest
   All in this mournful plight ?

From London I came, the damsel reply'd,
   From London upon the Thames,
Which circled is, O grief to tell !
   Besieg'd with foreign arms,

By the proud prince of Arragon,
   Who swears by his martial hand
To have the princèss to his spouse,
   Or else to waste this land ;

Except such champions can be found,
   That dare fight three to three,
Against the prince, and giants twain,
   Most horrid for to see ;

Whose grisly looks, and eyes like brands,
   Strike terrour where they come,
With serpents hissing on their helms,
   Instead of feathered plume.

K

The princess shall be the victor's prize,
    The king hath vow'd and said,
And he that shall the conquest win,
    Shall have her to his bride.

Now we are four damsels sent abroad,
    To the east, west, north, and south,
To try whose fortune is so good
    To find these champions forth.

But all in vain we have sought about,
    For none so bold there are
That dare adventure life and blood,
    To free a lady fair.

When is the day? quoth Robin Hood,
    Tell me this and no more.
On Midsummer next, the dam'sel said,
    Which is June the twenty-four.

With that the tears trickled down her cheeks,
    And silent was her tongue :
With sighs and sobs she took her leave,
    Away her palfrey sprung.

This news struck Robin to the heart,
    He fell down on the grass,
His actions and his troubled mind
    Shew'd he perplexed was.

Where lies your grief? quoth Will Scadlock,
    O master, tell to me :
If the damsel's eyes have pierc'd your heart,
    I'll fetch her back to thee.

Now nay, now nay, quoth Robin Hood,
    She doth not cause my smart ;
But 'tis the poor distress'd princess,
    That wounds me to the heart :

I will go fight the giants all
    To set the lady free.
The devil take my soul, quoth Little John,
    If I part with thy company.

Must I stay behind? quoth Will Scadlòck,
    No, no, that must not be ;
I'le make the third man in the fight.
    So we shall be three to three.

These words cheer'd Robin to the heart,
    Joy shone within his face,
Within his arms he hugg'd them both,
    And kindly did imbrace.

Quoth he, we'll put on mothly gray,
    And long staves in our hands,
A scrip and bottle by our sides,
    As come from the holy land.

So may we pass along the high-way,
    None will ask from whence we.came,
But take us pilgrims for to be,
    Or else some holy men.

Now they are on their journey gone,
    As fast as they may speed,
Yet for all haste, ere they arriv'd,
    The princess forth was led,

To be deliver'd to the prince,
    Who in the lists did stand,
Prepar'd to fight, or else receive
    His lady by the hand.

With that·he walked about the lists,
    With giants by his side :
Bring forth, said he, your champions,
    Or bring me forth my bride.

This is the four and twentieth day,
The day prefixt upon :
Bring forth my bride, or London burns,
I swear by Acaron.*

* Acaron. This termagant prince seems intended for
a sort of Mahometan Pagan; but Arragon, at least the
county of Arragon, was never in the hands of the Moors,
and there has been a succession of *Christian Kings* from the
year 1034. *Alcoran* is a deity formed by metathesis from
Alcoran, a book. This conversion is much more ancient
than the present ballad. Thus, in the old metrical romance
of *The sowdon of Babyloyne*, a MS. in the possession of
Dr. Farmer :

> " When Laban herde of this myschief,
>   A sory man was he,
> He trumped his men to relefe,
>   For to cease that tyme mente he,
>   Mersadage kinge of Barbarye
> He did carye to his tente,
>   And beryed him by right of Sarsenye,
> With brennynge fire and rich oynemente ;
>   And songe the *dirige* of ALKARON,
>   *That bibill is of here laye ;*
> And wayled his deth everyehon,
>   Seven nygatis and seven dayes."

Here *Alkaron* is expressly the name of a BOOK (*i.e.* the
Koran or *Alcoran*); in the following passage it is that of a
GOD :

> " Now shall ye here of Laban :
>   Whan tidynges to him were comen,
> Tho was he a fulle sory man,
>   Whan he herde how his vitaile were nomen,
>   And how his men were slayne,
>   And Gyc was go safe hem froo ;
> He defyed *Mahounde*, and *Apolyne*,
>   *Jubiter, Astarot*, and *Alcaran* also."

Wynken de Worde printed "A lytell treatyse of the
Turkes law called Alcaron, &c." See Herbert, 224. It
was a proper name in the East; as "Accaron princeps
insulæ Cypri," is mentioned by Roger de Hoveden, 786.—
Ritson.

Then cries the king, and queen likewise,
    Both weeping as they speake,
Lo! we have brought our daughter dear,
    Whom we are forc'd to forsake.

With that stept out bold Robin Hood,
    Crys, my liege, it must not be so:
Such beauty as the fair princèss
    Is not for a tyrant's mow.

The prince he then began to storm,
    Cries, fool, fanatick, baboon! *
How dare you stop my valour's prize?
    I'll kill thee with a frown.

Thou tyrant Turk, thou infidel,
    Thus Robin began to reply,
Thy frowns I scorn; lo! here's my gage,
    And thus I thee defie.

And for those two Goliahs there,
    That stand on either side,
Here are two little Davids by,
    That soon can tame their pride.

Then did the king for armour send,
    For lances, swords, and shields;
And thus all three in armour bright,
    Came marching to the field.

The trumpets 'gan to sound a charge,
    Each singled out his man;
Their arms in pieces soon were hew'd,
    Blood sprang from every vein.

The prince he reacht Robin Hood a blow,
    He struck with might and main,

* For *fanatick, baboon!* we should probably read '*fran tick*' baboon!—*Ritson*.

Which forc'd him to reel about the field,
  As though he had been slain.

God-a-mercy, quoth Robin, for that blow !
  The quarrel shall soon be try'd ;
This stroke shall shew a full divorce
  Betwixt thee and thy bride.

So from his shoulders he's cut his head,
  Which on the ground did fall,
And grumbling sore at Robin Hood,
  To be so dealt withal.

The giants then began to rage
  To see their prince lie dead :
Thou's be the next, quoth little John,
  Unless thou well guard thy head.

With that his faulchion he whirl'd about,
  It was both keen and sharp ;
He clove the giant to the belt,
  And cut in twain his heart.

Will Scadlock well had play'd his part,
  The giant he had brought to his knee ;
Quoth Will, the devil can't break his fast,
  Unless he have you all three.

So with his faulchion he run him through,
  A deep and gashly wound ;
Who damn'd and foam'd, curst and blasphem'd,
  And then fell to the ground.

Now all the lists with shouts were fill'd,
  The skies they did resound
Which brought the princess to herself,
  Who had fal'n in a swound.

The king and queen, and princess fair,
  Came walking to the place,

And gave the champions many thanks,
  And did them further grace.

Tell me, quoth the king, whence you are,
  That thus disguised came,
Whose valour speaks that noble blood
  Doth run through every vein.

A boon, a boon, quoth Robin Hood,
  On my knees I beg and crave ;
By my crown, quoth the king, I grant,
  Ask what, and thou shalt have.

Then pardon I beg for my merry men,
  Which are in the green-wood,
For Little John, and Will Scadlock,
  And for me bold Robin Hood.

Art thou Robin Hood ? then quoth the king,
  For the valour you have shewn,
Your pardons I do freely grant,
  And welcome every one.

The princess I promis'd the victor's prize,
  She cannot have you all three.
She shall chuse, quoth Robin.   Saith Little John,
  Then little share falls to me.

Then did the princess view all three,
  With a comely lovely grace,
And took Will Scadlock by the hand,
  Saying, here I make my choice.

With that a noble lord stept forth,
  Of Maxfield earl was he,
Who lookt Will Scadlock in the face,
  And wept most bitterly.

Quoth he, I had a son like thee,
  Whom I lov'd wondrous well,

But he is gone, or rather dead,
  His name it is young Gamwell.
Then did Will Scadlock fall on his knees,
  Cries, father! father! here,
Here kneels your son, your young Gamwell,
  You said you lov'd so dear.

But, lord! what imbracing and kissing was there,
  When all these friends were met!
They are gone to the wedding, and so to bedding:
  And so I bid you good night.

THE JOLLY PINDER OF WAKEFIELD,

WITH ROBIN HOOD, SCARLET, AND JOHN.

FROM an old black-letter copy, in A. à Wood's Collection,
compared with two other copies in the British Museum,
one in black-letter. It should be sung "To an excellent
tune," which has not been recovered.

Several lines of this ballad are quoted in two old plays
of the "Downfall" and "Death of Robert earle of Huntington," 1601, 4to. b. l. but acted many years before. It
is also alluded to in Shakspere's "Merry Wives of Windsor,"
act i. scene 1, and again, in his "Second Part of King Hen.
IV." act v. scene 3. In 1557 certain "ballets" are entered
on the books of the Stationers' Company "to John Wallye
and Mrs. Toye," one of which is entitled "Of Wakefylde
and a grene;" meaning apparently the ballad here re-
printed.

In Wakefield there lives a jolly pindèr,*
  In Wakefield all on a green,
  In Wakefield all on a green :
There is neither knight nor squire, said the pindèr,
  Nor baron that is so bold,
  Nor baron that is so bold,
Dare make a trespàss to the town of Wakefield,
  But his pledge goes to the pinfold, &c.

* Formerly written pinner, *i.e.* one who takes care of
cattle in the pound. "Pynner or empounder of cattel;"
Inclusor.—Howlett's "Abecedarium."—*Douce*.

All this beheard three wighty yeomen,*
    'Twas Robin Hood, Scarlet and John ;†
With that they espy'd the jolly pindèr,
    As he sat under a thorn.

Now turn again, turn again, said the pindèr,
    For a wrong way you have gone ;
For you have forsaken the king's highway,
    And made a path over the corn.

O that were a shame, said jolly Robìn,
    We being three, and thou but one.
The pinder leapt back then thirty good foot,
    'Twas thirty good foot and one.

He leaned his back fast unto a thorn,
    And his foot against a stone,
And there he fought a long summer's day,
    A summer's day so long,
Till that their swords on their broad bucklèrs,
    Were broke fast into their hands.

Hold thy hand, hold thy hand, said bold Robin
    Hood,
    And my merry men stand aside ;
For this is one of the best pindèrs,‡
    That with sword ever I tryed.

---

* In an edition among the Roxburgh ballads, the Editor finds "wight yeomen," instead of witty young men ; a far preferable reading ; wight, being the Saxon for active, swift, "of hem that ben deliver and wight."—*Conf. Am.* 177 b.

† In Shakspere's "Henry IV." part ii. the concluding line, before the command "to carry Master Silence to bed," he hums a scrap taken from this ballad.

‡ This is the reading in one black-letter copy that has come under the Editor's notice, instead of
    " For this is one of the best pinders
    That ever I tried with sword "

And wilt thou forsake thy pinder's craft,
  And go to the greenwood with me ?
Thou shalt have a livery twice in the year,
  Th' one greene, 'tither brown shall be.*

Then I'le take my blew blade all in my hand,
  And plod to the green-wood with thee.
Hast thou either meat or drink, said Robin Hood,
  For my merry men and me ?

I have both bread and beef, said the pindèr,
  And good ale of the best.
And that is meat good enough, said Robin Hood,
  For such unbidden guest.

O wilt thou forsake the pinder his craft,
  And go to the green-wood with me ;
Thou shalt have a livery twice in the year,
  The one green, the other brown.

If Michaelmas day was come and gone,
  And my master had paid me my fee,
Then would I set as little by him,
  As my master doth by me.

* In the black-letter ballad last alluded to, these lines
are certainly an improvement upon the following in Ritson's
edition :—

  " At Michaelmas next my cov'nant comes out,
    When every man gathers his fee."

ROBIN HOOD AND THE BISHOP.

SHOWING how Robin Hood went to an old woman's house
and changed cloaths with her to scape from the bishop;
and how he robbed the bishop of all his gold, and made
him sing a mass. To the tune of Robin Hood and the
Stranger. From an old black-letter copy in the Collection
of Anthony à Wood.—*Ritson.*

Compared by the Editor with one in the Roxburgh
Collection.

COME, gentlemen all, and listen awhile,
               Hey down, down, an a down,
  And a story Ile to you unfold ;
Ile tell you how Robin Hood served the bishop,
  When he robb'd him of his gold.

As it fell out on a sun-shining day,
  When Phœbus was in his prime,
Bold Robin Hood, that archer good,
  In mirth would spend some time.

And as he walk'd the forrest along,
  Some pastime for to spy,
There was he aware of a proud bishop,
  And all his company.

O what shall I do, said Robin Hood then,
  If the bishop he doth take me ?
No mercy he'l show unto me, I know,
  But hangèd I shall be.

'Then Robin was stout, and turn'd him about,
   And a little house there did he spy ;
And to an old wife, to save his life,
   He aloud began to cry.

Why, who art thou ? said the old woman,
   Come tell it to me for good.
I am an out-law, as many do know,
   My name it is Robin Hood ;

And yonder's the bishop and all his men,
   And if that I taken be,
Then day and night he'l work my spight,
   And hangèd I shall be.

If thou be Robin Hood, said the old womàn,
   As thou dost seem to be,
I'le for thee provide, and thee I will hide,
   From the bishop and his company.

For I remember one Saturday night,
   Thou brought me both shoes and hose ;
Therefore I'le provide thy person to hide,
   And keep thee from thy foes.

Then give me soon thy coat of grey,
   And take thou my mantle of green ;
Thy spindle and twine unto me resign,
   And take thou my arrows so keen.

And when Robin Hood was thus arraid,
   He went straight to his company,
With his spindle and twine, he oft lookt behind
   For the bishop and his company.

O who is yonder, quoth Little John,
   That now comes over the lee ?
An arrow at her I will let flie,
   So like an old witch looks she.

O hold thy hand, hold thy hand, said Robin
    Hood then,
And shoot not thy arrows so keen ;
I am Robin Hood, thy master good,
    And quickly it shall be seen.

The bishop he came to the old woman's house,
    And called with furious mood,
Come let me soon see, and bring unto me
    That traytor Robin Hood.

The old woman he set on a milk-white steed,
    Himselfe on a dapple gray ;
And for joy he had got Robin Hood,
    He went laughing all the way.

But as they were riding the forrest along,
    The bishop he chanc'd for to see
A hundred brave bowmen bold,
    Stand under the green-wood tree.

O who is yonder, the bishop then said,
    That's ranging within yonder wood ?
Marry, says the old woman, I think it to be
    A man call'd Robin Hood.

Why, who art thou, the bishop he said,
    Which I have here with me ?
Why, I am an old woman, thou cuckoldy bishop,
    Lift up my leg and see.

Then woe is me, the bishop he said,
    That ever I saw this day !
He turn'd him about, but Robin Hood stood,
    Call'd to him, and bid him stay.

Then Robin took hold of the bishop's horse,
    And ty'd him fast to a tree ;

Then Little John smil'd his master upon,
    For joy of this company.

Robin Hood took his mantle from 's back,
    And spread it upon the ground,
And out of the bishop's portmantle he
    Soon told five hundred pound.

Now let him go, said Robin Hood ;
    Said Little John, that may not be ;
For I vow and protest he shall sing us a mass,
    Before that he goe from me.

Then Robin Hood took the bishop by the hand,
    And bound him fast to a tree,
And made him sing a mass, God wot,
    To him and his yeomandry.

And then they brought him through the wood,
    And set him on his dapple gray,
And gave him the tail within his hand,
    And bade him for Robin Hood pray.

ROBIN HOOD AND THE BUTCHER.

FROM Anthony à Wood's Collection; there is also a copy
of it in the Royal Collection at the British Museum.

COME, all you brave gallants, and listen awhile,
          With hey down, down, an a down,
  That are this bower within :
For of Robin Hood, that archer good,
  A song I intend to sing.

Upon a time it chancèd so,
  Bold Robin in the forest did 'spy,
A jolly butchèr, with a bonny fine mare,
  With his flesh to the market did hye.

Good morrow, good fellow, said jolly Robìn,
  What food hast thou, tell unto me ?
Thy trade to me tell, and where thou dost dwell,
  For I like well thy company.

The butcher he answer'd jolly Robìn,
  No matter where I dwell ;
For a butcher I am, and to Nottinghàm
  I am going, my flesh to sell.

What's the price of thy flesh ? said jolly Robìn,
  Come tell it soon unto me ;
And the price of thy mare, be she never so dear,
  For a butcher fain would I be.

The price of my flesh, the butcher reply'd,
  I soon will tell unto thee ;
With my bonny mare, and they are not dear,
  Four mark thou must give unto me.

Four mark I will give thee, saith jolly Robin,
  Four mark it shall be thy fee ;
The money come count, and let me mount,
  For a butcher I fain would be.

Now Robin he is to Nottingham gone,
  His butcher's trade to begin ;
With good intent to the sheriff he went,
  And there he took up his inne.

When other butchers did open their meat,
  Bold Robin he then begun ;
But how for to sell he knew not well,
  For a butcher he was but young.

When other butchers no meat could sell
  Robin got both gold and fee ;
For he sold more meat for one peny
  Than others could do for three.

But when he sold his meat so fast,
  No butcher by him could thrive ;
For he sold more meat for one peny
  Than others could do for five.

Which made the butchers of Nottingham
  To study as they did stand,
Saying, surely he was some prodigal,
  That hath sold his father's land.

The butchers stepp'd to jolly Robin,
  Acquainted with him for to be ;
Come, brother, one said, we be all of one trade,
  Come, will you go dine with me ?

L

Accurst of his heart, said jolly Robin,
  That a butcher will deny ;
I will go with you, my brethren true,
  And as fast as I can hie.

But when to the sheriff's house they came,
  To dinner they hied apace,
And Robin Hood he the man must be
  Before them all to say grace.

Pray God bless us all, said jolly Robin,
  And our meat within this place ;
A cup of sack so good will nourish our blood :
  And so do I end my grace.

Come fill us more wine, said jolly Robin,
  Let us be merry while we do stay ;
For wine and good cheer, be it never so dear,
  I vow I the reck'ning will pay.

Come, brothers, be merry, said jolly Robin,
  Let us drink, and never give ore ;
For the shot I will pay, ere I go my way,
  If it cost me five pounds and more.

This is a mad blade, the butchers then said,
  Saies the sheriff, he is some prodigàl,
That some land hath sold for silver and gold,
  And now he doth mean to spend all.

Hast thou any horn beasts, the sheriff repli'd,
  Good fellow, to sell unto me ;
"Yes, that I have, good master sheriff,
  I have hundreds two or three,

And a hundred aker of good free land,
  If you please it to see :
And Ile make you as good assurance of it,
  As ever my father made me."

The sheriff he saddled his good palfrèy,
  And, with three hundred pound in gold,
Away he went with bold Robin Hood,
  His horned beasts to behold.

Away then the sheriff and Robin did ride,
  To the forrest of merry Sherwood,
Then the sheriff did say, God bless us this day,
  From a man they call Robin Hood !

But when a little farther they came,
  Bold Robin he chancèd to spy
A hundred head of good red deer,
  Come tripping the sheriff full nigh.

"How like you my horn'd beasts, good master
    sheriff ?
  They be fat and fair for to see."
"I tell thee, good fellow, I would I were gone,
  For I like not thy company."

Then Robin set his horn to his mouth,
  And blew but blasts three :
Then quickly anon there came Little John,
  And all his company.

What is your will, master ? then said Little John,
  Good master come tell unto me ;
"I have brought hither the sheriff of Nottingham
  This day to dine with thee."

He is welcome to me, then said Little John,
  I hope he will honestly pay ;
I know he has gold, if it be but well told,
  Will serve us to drink a whole day.

Then Robin took his mantle from his back,
  And laid it upon the ground :

And out of the sheriff's portmantle
  He told three hundred pound.

Then Robin brought him through the wood,
  And set him on his dapple gray ;
" O have me commended to your wife at home :"
  So Robin went laughing away.

ROBIN HOOD'S RESCUING WILL STUTLY.

From Anthony à Wood's Collection ; the full title being, "Robin Hood his rescuing Will Stutly from the Sheriff and his men, who had taken him prisoner, and was going to hang him."

WHEN Robin Hood in the green wood liv'd,
  Derry, derry down,
 Under the green wood tree,
Tidings there came to him with speed,
  Tidings for certainty.
    Hey down, derry, derry, down.

That Will Stutly surprised was,
 And eke in prison lay ;
Three varlets that the sheriff had hired,
 Did likely him betray ;

Aye, and to-morrow hanged must be,
 To-morrow as soon as it is day ;
Before they could this victory get,
 Two of them would Stutly slay.

When Robin Hood he heard this news,
 Lord ! it did grieve him sore ;
And to his merry men he said,
 (Who altogether swore)

That Will Stutly should rescued be,
 And be brought back again ;
Or else should many a gallant wight
 For his sake there be slain.

He cloathed himself in scarlet then,
  His men were all in green ;
A finer shew, throughout the world,
  In no place could be seen.

Good lord ! it was a gallant sight
  To see them all on a row ;
With every man a good broad sword,
  And eke a good yew bow.

Forth of the green wood are they gone,
  Yea all courageously,
Resolving to bring Stutly home,
  Or every man to die.

And when they came to the castle neer,
  Whereas Will Stutly lay,
I hold it good, saith Robin Hood,
  We here in ambush stay,

And send one forth some news to hear,
  To yonder palmer fair,
That stands under the castle wall,
  Some news he may declare.

With that steps forth a brave young man,
  Which was of courage bold,
Thus he did say to the old man,
  I pray thee, palmer old,

Tell me, if that thou rightly ken,
  When must Will Stutly die,
Who is one of bold Robin's men,
  And here doth prisoner lie ?

Alack ! alass ! the palmer said,
  And for ever wo is me !
Will Stutly hanged will be this day,
  On yonder gallows tree.

O had his noble master known,
  He would some succour send ;
A few of his bold yeomandree
  Full soon would fetch him hence.

Ay, that is true, the young man said ;
  Ay, that is true, said he ;
Or, if they were near this place,
  They soon would set him free.

But fare thou well, thou good old man,
  Farewell, and thanks to thee ;
If Stutly hanged be this day,
  Reveng'd his death will be.

No sooner hee was from the palmer gone,
  But the gates were open'd wide,
And out of the castle Will Stutly came,
  Guarded on every side.

When hee was forth of the castle come,
  And saw no help was nigh,
Thus he did say unto the sheriff,
  Thus he said gallantly :

Now seeing that I needs must die,
  Grant me one boon, said he,
For my noble master nere had a man,
  That yet was hang'd on tree.

Give me a sword all in my hand,
  And let mee be unbound,
And with thee and thy men Ile fight,
  Till I lie dead on the ground.

But this desire he would not grant,
  His wishes were in vain ;
For the sheriff swore he hanged should be,
  And not by the sword be slain.

Do but unbind my hands, he saies,
   I will no weapons crave,
And if I hanged be this day,
   Damnation let me have.

O no, O no, the sheriff said,
   Thou shalt on the gallows die,
Ay, and so shall thy master too,
   If ever in me it lie.

O, dastard coward! Stutly cries,
   Faint-hearted pesant slave!
If ever my master do thee meet,
   Thou shall thy paiment have.

My noble master thee doth scorn,
   And all thy cowardly crew;
Such silly imps unable are
   Bold Robin to subdue.

But when he was to the gallows come,
   And ready to bid adiew,
Out of a bush leaps little John,
   And goes Will Stutly to:

"I pray thee, Will, before thou die,
   Of thy dear friends take leave;
I needs must borrow him a while,
   How say you, master shrieve?"

Now, as I live, the sheriff said,
   That varlet will I know;
Some sturdy rebell is that same,
   Therefore let him not go.

Then Little John most hastily
   Away cut Stutly's bands,
And from one of the sheriffs men,
   A sword twicht from his hands.

"Here, Will Stutly, take this same,
  Thou canst it better sway ;
And here defend thyself awhile,
  For aid will come straightway."

And there they turned them back to back,
  In the midst of them that day,
Till Robin Hood approached near,
  With many an archer gay.

With that an arrow from them flew,
  I wist from Robin Hood ;
Make haste, make haste, the sheriff he said,
  Make haste, for it is not good.

The sheriff is gon ; his doughty men
  Thought it no boot to stay,
But as their master had them taught,
  They run full fast away.

O stay, O stay, Will Stutly said,
  Take leave ere you depart ;
You neere will catch bold Robin Hood,
  Unless you dare him meet.

O ill betide you, quoth Robin Hood,
  That you so soon are gone ;
My sword may in the scabbard rest,
  For here our work is done.

I little thought, Will Stutly said,
  When I came to this place,
For to have met with Little John,
  Or seen my master's face.

Thus Stutly was at liberty set,
  And safe brought from his foe :
"O thanks, O thanks to my master,
  Since here it was not so.

And once again, my fellows dear,
 We shall in the green woods meet,
Where we shall make our bow-strings twang
 Musick for us most sweet."
                    Hey down, &c.

The Song of Robin Hood and his Huntes-men.—P. 155.

ROBIN HOOD AND THE BEGGAR:

SHOWING how Robin Hood and the Beggar fought, and
how he changed cloaths with the Beggar, and how he
went a begging to Nottingham: and how he saved three
brethren from being hang'd for stealing of the king's deer.
To the tune of Robin Hood and the Stranger.

From an old black-letter copy in the Collection of
Anthony à Wood, compared with the Roxburgh copy.

The Editor was unwilling to add any more to the sixteen
ballads which composed the first edition of the garland,
by the insertion of another version of Robin Hood and
the Beggar, which appears in the first volume of Ritson,
and which will be found in a subsequent page of this
volume.

COME light and listen, you gentlemen all,
　　　　　Hey down, down, an a down,
That mirth do love for to hear,
And a story true Ile tell unto you,
　　If that you will but draw near.

In elder times, when merriment was,
　　And archery was holden good,
There was an outlàw as many did know,
　　Which men called Robin Hood.

Upon a time it chanced so,
　　Bold Robin was merry dispos'd,
His time to spend he did intend,
　　Either with friend or foe.

Then he got upon a gallant fine steed,
  The which was worth angels ten,
With a mantle of green, most brave to be seen,
  He left all his merry men.

And riding towards Nottingham,
  Some pastime for to 'spy,
There was he aware of a jolly beggàr,
  As ere he beheld with his eye.

An old patch'd coat the beggar had on,
  Which he daily did use to wear ;
And many a bag about him did wag,
  Which made Robin to him repair.

God speed, God speed, said Robin Hood,
  What countryman ? tell unto me.
"I am Yorkshire, sir, but ere you go far,
  Some charity give unto me."

Why, what wouldst thou have ? said Robin Hood,
  I pray thee tell unto me.
No lands nor livings, the beggar he said,
  But a penny for charitie.

I have no money, said Robin Hood then,
  But a ranger within the wood ;
I am an outlaw, as many do know,
  My name it is Robin Hood.

But yet I must tell thee, bonny beggàr,
  That a bout with thee I must try ;
Thy coat of gray, lay down I say,
  And my mantle of green shall lye by.

Content, content, the beggar he cry'd,
  Thy part it will be the worse ;
For I hope this bout to give thee the rout,
  And then have at thy purse.

The beggar he had a mickle long staffe,
    Robin had a nut-brown sword ;
So the beggar drew nigh, and at Robin let fly
    But gave him never a word.

Fight on, fight on, said Robin Hood then,
    This game well pleaseth me.
For every blow Robin then did give,
    The beggar gave buffets three.

And fighting there full hard and sore,
    Not far from Nottingham town,
They never fled, till from Robin Hood's head
    The blood came trickling down.

O, hold thy hand, said Robin Hood then,
    And thou and I will agree.
If that be true, the beggar he said,
    Thy mantle come give unto me.

Nay, a change, a change, cried Robin Hood,
    Thy bags and coat give me ;
And this mantle of mine Ile to thee resign,
    My horse and my braverye.

When Robin had got the beggar's cloaths,
    He lookèd round about ;
Methinks, said he, I seem to be
    A beggar brave and stout.

For now I have a bag for my bread,
    So have I another for corn ;
I have one for salt, and another for malt,
    And one for my little horn.

And now I will a begging goe,
    Some charitie for to find.
And if any more of Robin you'll know,
    In the second part it's behind.

[THE SECOND PART.]

Now Robin he is to Nottingham gone,
                Hey down, down, an a down,
  With his bag hanging down to his knee,
His staff, and his coat, scarce worth a groat,
  Yet merrilie passed he.

As Robin he pass'd the streets along,
  He heard a pittiful cry ;
Three brethren dear, as he did hear,
  Condemned were to dye.

Then Robin he highed to the sheriffs,
  Some reliefe for to seek ;
He skipt, and he leapt, and caper'd full high,
  As he went along the street.

But when to the sheriff's doore he came,
  He met a gentleman fine and brave,
Though beggar, said he, come tell unto me
  What is it thou wouldest have.

No meat, nor drink, said Robin Hood then,
  That I come here to crave ;
But to get the lives of youg men three,
  And that I fain would have.

That cannot be, thou bold beggàr,
  Their fact it is so clear ;
I tell to thee, they hang'd must be,
  For stealing of the king's deer.

But when to the gallows they did come,
  There was many a weeping eye :
O, hold your peace, said Robin Hood then,
  For certainly they shall not dye.

Then Robin he set his horn to his mouth,
　And he blew out blastes three,
Till a hundred bold archers brave
　Came kneeling down to his knee.

What is your will, mastèr ? they said,
　We are here at your command.
Shoot east, shoot west, said Robin Hood then,
　And see you spare no man.

Then they shot east, then they shot west.
　Their arrows were so keen ;
The sheriffe he, and his companie,
　No longer must be seen.

Then he stept to those brethren three,
　And away he has them ta'ne ;
The sheriffe was crost, and many a man lost,
　That dead lay on the plain.

And away they went into the merry green wool,
　And sung with a merry glee ;
Then Robin Hood took these brethren good
　To be of his yeomandrie.

ROBIN HOOD AND QUEEN KATHERINE.

FROM an old black-letter copy in a private collection, compared with another in that of Anthony à Wood. The full title is: "Renowned Robin Hood; or, his famous archery truly related in the worthy exploits he acted before queen Katherine, he being an outlaw man; and how he obtained his own and his fellows pardon. To a new tune."

It is scarcely worth observing that there was no queen consort named Katherine before Henry the Fifth's time: but as Henry the Eighth had no less than three wives so called, the name would be sufficiently familiar to our balladmaker.—*Ritson.* The copy in the Roxburgh Collection, with which this has been compared, is divided into two parts, the second commencing with the 75th stanza, " What is the wager? said the Queen ;" and from this copy the Editor has made several emendations or corrections.

GOLD tane from the kings harbengers,
        Downe, a downe, a downe,
  As seldome hath beene scene,
        Downe, a downe, a downe,
And carried by bold Robin Hood
  For a present to the queene,
        Downe, a downe, a downe,

If that I live a yeare to an end,
  Thus did queene Katherine say,
Bold Robin Hood, I will be thy friend,
  And all thy yeomen gay.

Robin Hood and Queen Katherine.—P. 160.

The queene is to her chamber gone,
   As fast as she can wen;
She calls unto her lovely page,
   His name was Richard Patrington.

Come thou hither to mee, thou lovely page,
   Come thou hither to mee;
For thou must post to Nottingham,
   As fast as thou can dree;

And as thou goest to Nottingham,
   Search all the English wood,
Enquire of one good yeoman or another,
   That can tell thee of Robin Hood.

Sometimes he went, sometimes he ran,
   As fast as he could win;
And when he came to Nottingham,
   There he tooke up his inn.

And when he came to Nottingham,
   And had tooke up his inne,
He calls for a bottle of Rhenish wine,
   And dranke a health to his queene.

There sate a yeoman by his side,
   Tell mee, sweet page, tell me,
What is thy businesse and thy cause,
   So far in the north countrey?

This is my businesse and the cause,
   Sir, I'le tell it you for good,
To enquire of one good yeoman or another,
   To tell mee of Robin Hood.

I'le get my horse betimes in the morne,
   Be it by break of day,
And I will shew thee bold Robin Hood,
   And all his yeomen gay.

When that he came at Robin Hood's place,
    He fell down on his knee ;
"Queen Katherine she doth greet you well,
    She greets you well by me ;

She bids you post to fair London court,
    Not fearing any thing :
For there shall be a little sport,
    And she hath sent you her ring."

Robin Hood tooke his mantle from his back,
    It was of the Lincolne greene,
And sent it by this lovely page,
    For a present unto the queene.

In summer time, when leaves grow green,
    'Twas a seemely sight to see,
How Robin Hood himselfe had drest,
    And all his yeomandry.

He clothed his men in Lincolne greene,
    And himselfe in scarlet red ;
Black hats, white feathers, all alike,
    Now bold Robin Hood is rid :

And when he came at London's court,
    He fell downe on his knee.
Thou art welcome, Locksly, said the queen,
    And all thy good yeomandree.

The king is into Finsbury field,*
    Marching in battle ray,†

---

* Ground near Moorfields, London, famous in old times
for the archery practised there. " In the year 1498," says
Stow, "all the gardens which had continued time out of
minde, without Mooregate, to wit, about and beyond the
lordship of Fensberry, were destroyed. And of them was
made a plaine field for archers to shoote in." Survay of
London, 1598, p. 351. See also p. 77, where it is observed

And after follows bold Robin Hood,
And all his yeomen gay.

Come hither, Tepus, said the king,
Bow-bearer after me ;
Come measure me out with this line,
How long our mark must be.

that "about the feast of St. Bartlemew . . . the officers
of the city . . . were challengers of all men in the
suburbes, . . . before the lord maior, aldermen, and
sheriffes, in FENSBERY FIELDE, to shoote the standarde,
broade arrow, and flight, for games." There is a tract
entitled, "Ayme for Finsburie archers, or an alphabetical
table of the names of every marke within the same fields,
with the true distances, both by the map, and dimensura-
tion with the line. Published for the ease of the skilfull,
and behoofe of the yoonge beginners in the famous ex-
cercise of archerie, by J. J. and E. B. To be sold at the
signe of the Swan in Grub-street, by F. Sergeant, 1594,
16mo. Republished by R. F. 1604 ; and again by James
Partridge, 1628. 12mo.
The practice of shooting here is alluded to by Cotton, in
his *Virgile travestie;* (b. iv.) 1667 :

  " And arrows loos'd from Grub-street bow,
    In FINSBURY, to him are slow ;"

and is said to have continued till within the memory of
persons now living. These famous archers are also mentioned by Ben Jonson in *Every man in his humour* (act i.
scene 1): " Because I dwell at Hogsden, I shall keep company with none but *the archers of Finsbury.*"
  † *Battle ray,* Battle array. The same expression occurs
in "The tragicall history of Didaco and Violenta," 1567 :

  " To traverse forth his grounde, to place
    His troupes *in butayle ray.*"

[THE SECOND PART.]

What is the wager ? said the queene,
   That must I now know here.
"Three hundred tun of Rhenish wine,
   Three hundred tun of beere ;
Three hundred of the fattest harts
   That run on Dallom lee."
That's a princely wager, said the king,
   That needs must I tell thee.

With that bespake one Clifton then,
   Full quickly and full soone :
Measure no markes for us, most soveraigne liege.
   Wee'l shoot at sun and moone.
"Ful fifteene score your marke shall be,
   Ful fifteene score shall stand."
I'll lay my bow, said Clifton then,
   I'll cleave the willow wand.

With that the king's archers led about,
   While it was three, or none ;
With that the ladies began to shout,
   "Madam, your game is gone."

A boone, a boone, queen Katherine cries,
   I crave it on my bare knee ;
Is there any knight of your privy counsel
   Of queen Katherine's part will be ?

Come hither to mee, sir Richard Lee,
   Thou art a knight full good :
For I do knowe by thy pedigree
   Thou sprung'st from Gower's blood.

Come hither to me, thou bishop of Hereford ;
  For a noble priest was hee.
By my silver miter, said the bishop then,
  Ile not bet one peny.

The king hath archers of his own,
  Full ready and full right,
And these be strangers every one,
  No man knowes what they hight.

What wilt thou bet ? said Robin Hood,
  Thou seest our game the worse.
By my silver miter, said the bishop then,
  All the money within my purse.

What is in thy purse ? said Robin Hood,
  Throw it downe on the ground.
Fifteen score nobles, said the bishop then ;
  It's neere an hundred pound.

Robin Hood took his bagge from his side,
  And threw it downe on the greene ;
William Scadlocke then went smiling away,
  " I know who this money must win."

With that the king's archers led about,
  While it was three and three ;
With that the ladies gave a shout,
  "Woodcock, beware thy knee !"

It is three and three, now, said the king,
  The next three pay for all.
Robin Hood went and whisper'd the queen,
  The king's part shall be but small.

Robin Hood hee led about,
  Hee shot it under hand ;
And Clifton with a bearing arrow,
  Hee clave the willow wand.

And little Midge, the miller's son,
    He shot not much the worse ;
He shot within a finger of the prick :
    "Now, bishop, beware thy purse !"

A boone, a boone, queen Katherine cries,
    I crave that on my bare knee,
That you will angry be with none
    That are of my partie.

They shall have forty daies to come,
    And forty daies to goe,
And three times forty to sport and play ;
    Then welcome friend or foe.

Thou art welcome, Robin Hood, said the queene
    And so is Little John,
And so is Midge, the miller's son ;
    Thrice welcome every one.

Is this Robin Hood ? now said the king ;
    For it was told to me
That he was slain in the palace gates,
    So far in the north country.

Is this Robin Hood ? quoth the bishop then,
    As I see well to be :
Had I knowne that had been that bold outlàw
    I would not have bet one peny.

Hee tooke me late one Saturday night, .
    And bound me fast to a tree,
And made me sing a masse, God wot,
    To him and his yeomandree.

What, an if I did, saies Robin Hood,
    Of that masse I was faine ;
For recompense to thee, he saies,
    Here's halfe thy gold againe.

Now nay, now nay, saies Little John,
 Master, that shall not be ;
We must give gifts to the king's officers
 That gold will serve thee and mee.

———

ROBIN HOOD AND THE TANNER;

OR, ROBIN HOOD MET WITH HIS MATCH.

A MERRY and pleasant song relating the gallant and fierce combate fought between Arthur Bland, a tanner of Nottingham, and Robin Hood, the greatest and most noblest archer of England. Tune is, Robin Hood and the Stranger. From an old black-letter copy in the Collection of Anthony à Wood.

There is an excellent ballad in "Percy's Reliques,' vol. ii. p. 91, called "King Edward the Fourth and the Tanner of Tamworth;" in which allusion is made to some of the localities in the Robin Hood ballads, but not sufficient to constitute, as the Editor conceives, a right of admission into this collection. The tale and incidents are totally distinct from this ballad of Robin Hood and the Tanner of Nottingham.

In Nottingham there lives a jolly tannèr,
　　With a hey down, down, a down, down,
　His name is Arthur-a-Bland ; *
There is nere a squire in Nottinghamshire
　Dare bid bold Arthur stand.

* Arthur-a-Bland, the tanner of Nottingham, says one of our ballad commentators, was a wild unsettled lad, and loved the hide better when rough and warm on the bull's back, than in his own tan pit, and in a fair way of becoming soles and uppers for boots and shoes. In his day there was no settled work for a tanner; husbandmen tanned the leather of their own shoes and horse furniture in a way which science would scorn now, but tough withal

Robin Hood and the Tanner.—P. 168.

With a long pike-staff upon his shoulder,
  So well he can clear his way ;
By two and by three he makes them to flee,
  For he hath no list to stay.

And as he went forth, in a summer's morning,
  Into the forrest of merry Sherwood,
To view the red-deer, that range here and there,
  There met he with bold Robin Hood.

As soon as bold Robin did him espy,
  He thought some sport he would make,
Therefore out of hand he bid him to stand,
  And thus to him he spake :

Why, what art thou, thou bold fellow,
  That ranges so boldly here ?
In sooth, to be brief, thou lookst like a thief,
  That comes to steal our king's deer.

For I am a keeper in this forrest,
  The king puts me in trust
To look to his deer, that range here and there ;
  Therefore stay thee I must.

" If thou beest a keeper in this forrest,
  And hast such a great command,
Yet thou must have more partakers * in store,
  Before thou make me to stand."

and wearable ; and this, perhaps, induced honest Arthur
to think more of Barnesdale Wood and his cousin Little
John than of toiling with raw hides in an unsavoury solu-
tion of oak bark and ditch water.   In this unsettled state
of mind, and with a reputation for a broil, he walked into
the forest prepared alike for mischief or mirth, careless
whether he met with a dun-deer or an armed outlaw.   In
colours suited to his character the ballad writer has admi-
rably sketched him.
  * Assistants, persons to take thy part.

" Nay, I have no more partakers in store,
  Or any that I do not need ;
But I have a staff of another oke graff,*
  I know it will do the deed.

For thy sword and thy bow I care not a straw,
  Nor all thy arrows to boot ;
If I get a knop† upon the bare scop, ‡
  Thou canst as well—as shoote."

Speak cleanly, good fellow, said jolly Robin,
  And give better terms to me ;
Else Ile thee correct for thy neglect,
  And make thee more mannerly.

Marry gep with a wenion !§ quoth Arthur-a-Bland,
  Art thou such a goodly man ?
I care not a fig for thy looking so big,
  Mend thou thyself where thou can.

---

* Oak-branch or sapling.
  † The knob, the top or end of a stick; thence applied
to a blow with a stick.
  ‡ Scalp, pate.
  § *Marry gep with a wenion.* [Mr. Ritson has left this
exclamation as a query, nor can we satisfactorily explain
it. *Marry* is the corruption of the oath "By St. Mary ;"
of *gep*, we know not the meaning: it may be a contraction
of *go up*, or *get up*, which appears not unlikely, as *Marry
come up* has been a common exclamation, and continues
yet in use; and both phrases are equivalent to Away !
Out with you ! still familiar terms.   *Wenion*, or *wanion* as
it is more commonly written, is not to be found in any of
the old dictionaries, and its exact meaning is uncertain:
it seems to be derived either from the Anglo-Saxon *wanung*,
detriment, or *wanian*, to deplore, to decrease, to fall away,
and to be equivalent to harm, evil, or sorrow ; and the
whole phrase to resolve itself into a hearty curse.—
  "With a wannion." A kind of execration. It occurs
in several old plays :--

Then Robin Hood he unbuckled his belt,
  And laid down his bow so long ;
He took up a staff of another oke graff,
  That was both stiff and strong.

I'le yield to thy weapon, said jolly Robin,
  Since thou wilt not yield to mine ;
For I have a staff of another oke graff,
  Not half a foot longer than thine.

But let me measure, said jolly Robin,
  Before we begin our fray ;
For I'le not have mine to be longer than thine,
  For that will be counted foul play.

I pass not for length, bold Arthur reply'd,
  My staff is of oke so free ;
Eight foot and a half, it will knock down a calf,
  And I hope it will knock down thee.

Then Robin could no longer forbear,
  He gave him such a knock,
Quickly and soon the blood came down,
  Before it was ten a clock.

Then Arthur he soon recover'd himself,
  And gave him such a knock on the crown,
That from every side of bold Robin Hood's head,
  The blood came trickling down.

Then Robin raged like a wild boar,
  As soon as he saw his own blood :

      " Look how thou stirrest now ; come away, or
      I'll fetch thee with a *wannion.*"—*Pericles.*

  " Where er he puts his head with a *wannion* a cuckold is,
  If his horns be forth, the devil's companion."
                  B. Jonson's Devil is an Ass.

  " Is here any work for Grace, *with a wannion* to her."
                  Davenport's City Nightcap.

Then Bland was in hast he laid on so fast,
    As though he had been cleaving of wood.

And about, and about, and about they went,
    Like two wild bores in a chase ;
Striving to aim each other to maim,
    Leg, arm, or any other place.

And knock for knock they lustily dealt,
    Which held for two hours and more ;
That all the wood rang at every bang,
    They ply'd their work so sore.

Hold thy hand, hold thy hand, said Robin Hood,
    And let thy quarrel fall ;
For here we may thrash our bones all to mesh,
    And get no coyn at all :

And in the forrest of merry Sherwood
    Hereafter thou shalt be free.
"God-a-mercy for nought, my freedom I bought,
    I may thank my staff, and not thee."

What tradesman art thou? said jolly Robin,
    Good fellow, I prethee me show :
And also me tell, in what place thou dost dwell?
    For both of these fain would I know.

I am a tanner, bold Arthur reply'd,
    In Nottingham long have I wrought ;
And if thou'lt come there, I vow and swear,
    I will tan thy hide for nought.

God-a-mercy, good fellow, said jolly Robin,
    Since thou art so kind and free ;
And if thou wilt tan my hide for nought, .
    I will do as much for thee.

And if thou'lt forsake thy tanner's trade,
    And live in the green wood with me,

My name's Robin Hood, I swear by the rood,
 I will give thee both gold and fee.

If thou be Robin Hood, bold Arthur reply'd,
 As I think well thou art,
Then here's my hand, my name is Arthur-a-Bland,
 We two will never depart.*

But tell me, O tell me, where is Little John ?
 Of him fain would I hear ;
For we are alide by the mother's side,
 And he is my kinsman dear.

Then Robin Hood blew on the beaugle horn,
 He blew full lowd and shrill ;
And quickly anon appear'd Little John,
 Come tripping down a green hill ;

O what is the matter ? then said Little John,
 Master, I pray you tell :
Why do you stand with your staff in your hand,
 I fear all is not well.

"O man I do stand, and he makes me to stand,
 The tanner that stands thee beside ;
Ile is a bonny blade, and master of his trade,
 For soundly he hath taun'd my hide."

He is to be commended, then said Little John,
 If such a feat he can do ;
If he be so stout, we will have a bout,
 And he shall tan my hide too.

Hold thy hand, hold thy hand, said Robin Hood,
 For as I do understand,
He s a yeoman good of thine own blood,
 For his name is Arthur-a-Bland.

---

 * Part *from* each other, separate.

Then Little John threw his staff away,
  As far as he could it fling,
And ran out of hand to Arthur-a-Bland,
  And about his neck did cling.

With loving respect, there was no neglect,
  They were neither nice nor coy,
Each other did face with a lovely grace,
  And both did weep for joy.

Then Robin Hood took them both by the hands,
  And danc'd round about the oke tree:
"For three merry men, and three merry men,
  And three merry men we be:

And ever hereafter as long as we live,
  We three will be as one;
The wood it shall ring, and the old wife sing,
  Of Robin Hood, Arthur, and John."

Robin Hood and the Curtal Fryer.—P. 175.

ROBIN HOOD AND THE CURTALL FRYER.

FROM an old black-letter copy in the Collection of Anthony
à Wood: corrected by a much earlier one in the Pepysian
Library, printed by H. Gosson, about the year 1610; compared with a later one in the same Collection. The full
title is: "The famous battell betweene Robin Hood and
the Curtall Fryer. . To a new Northerne tune."

Compared by the Editor with the Roxburgh ballads.

"The Curtall Fryer," Dr. Stukeley says, "is *cordelier*,
from the cord or rope which they wore round their waist,
to whip themselves with. They were," adds he, "of the
Franciscan order." Our fryer, however, is undoubtedly so
called from his "curtall dogs," or curs, as we now say.
(*Courtault*, F.) In fact, he is no fryer at all, but a monk
of Fountain's Abbey, which was of the Cistercian order.—
Ritson.

Mr. Douce, in his copy of Robin Hood, says also, that
the explanation of Dr. Stukeley is very unsatisfactory;
that of Staveley is much more probable, who in chap. xxv.
of his "Romish Horseleech," asserts, that in some countries
where the Franciscan Friars, conformably to the injunc-
tions of their founder, wore short habits, the order was
presently contemned and derided, and men called them
Curtailed Friars.

IN summer time, when leaves grow green,
    And flowers are fresh and gay,
Robin Hood and his merry men
    Were disposed to play.

Then some would leape, and some would runne,
    And some would use artillery;

"Which of you can a good bow draw,
 A good archèr to be?
Which of you can kill a bucke,
 Or who can kill a doe;
Or who can kill a hart of Greece*
 Five hundreth foot him fro?"

Will Scadlocke he did kill a bucke,
 And Midge he kild a doe;
And Little John kild a hart of Greece,
 Five hundreth foot him fro.

God's blessing on thy heart, said Robin Hood,
 That shot such a shot for me;
I would ride my horse a hundred miles,
 To find one could match thee.

This caused Will Scadlocke to laugh,
 He laught full heartily:
"There lives a curtall fryer in Fountaines Abbey
 Will beate both him and thee.

The curtall fryer in Fountaines Abbey
 Well can a strong bow draw,
He will beat you and your yeomèn,
 Set them all on a row."

Robin Hoode tooke a solemne oath,
 It was by Mary free,
That he would neither eate nor drinke,
 Till the fryer he did see.

Robin Hood put on his harnesse good,
 And on his head a cap of steel,
Broad sword and buckler by his side,
 And they became him weele.

* This means perhaps, no more than a fat hart, for the
sake of a quibble between Greece and *grease*.

He tooke his bow into his hand,
　It was made of a trusty tree,
With a sheafe of arrowes at his belt,
　And to Fountaine Dale went he.

And comming unto Fountaine Dale,
　No farther would he ride ;
There was he ware of the curtall fryer,
　Walking by the water side.

The fryer had on a harnesse good,
　And on his head a cap of steel,
Broad sword and buckler by his side,
　And they became him weele.

Robin Hood lighted off his horse,
　And tyed him to a thorne :
"Carry me over the water, thou curtall fryer,
　Or else thy life's forlorne."

The fryer tooke Robin Hood on his backe,
　Deepe water he did bestride,
And spake neither good word nor bad,
　Till he came at the other side.

Lightly leapt Robin offe the fryer's backe ;
　The fryer said to him againe,
Carry me over this water, thou fine fellow,
　Or it shall breed thy paine.

Robin Hood took the fryer on his backe,
　Deepe water he did bestride,
And spake neither good word nor bad,
　Till he came at the other side.

Lightly leapt the fryer off Robin Hood's backe,
　Robin Hood said to him againe,
Carry me over this water, thou curtall fryer,
　Or it shall breede thy pain.

N

Th« fryer tooke Robin on's backe againe,
   And stept in to the knee ;
Till he came at the middle streame,
   Neither good nor bad spake he ;

And coming to the middle streame,
   There he threw Robin in :
"And chuse thee, chuse thee, fine fellow,
   Whether thou wilt sink or swim."

Robin Hood swam to a bush of broome,
   The fryer to a wigger wand ;
Bold Robin Hood is gone to shore,
   And took his bow in his hand.

One of his best arrowes under his belt
   To the fryer he let fly ;
The curtall fryer with his steel buckler
   Did put that arrow by.

"Shoot on, shoot on, thou fine fellow,
   Shoot as thou hast begun,
If thou shoot here a summer's day,
   Thy marke I will not shun."

Robin Hood shot passing well,
   Till all his arrows were gane ;
They tooke their swords and steele bucklers,
   They fought with might and maine,

From ten o'th' clock that very day,
   Till four i'th' afternoon ;
Then Robin Hood came to his knees,
   Of the fryer to beg a boone.

"A boone, a boone, thou curtall fryer,
   I beg it on my knee ;
Give me leave to set my horne to my mouth,
   And to blow blasts three."

That I will do, said the curtall fryer,
  Of thy blasts I have no doubt;
I hope thou'lt blow so passing well,
  Till both thy eyes fall out.

Robin Hood set his horne to his mouth,
  He blew out blasts three;
Halfe a hundreth yeomen, with bowes bent,
  Came raking over the lee.

Whose men are these, said the fryer,
  They come so hastily?
Those are mine, said Robin Hood;
  Fryer, what is that to thee?

A boone, a boone, said the curtall fryer,
  The like I gave to thee;
Give me leave to set my fist to my mouth,
  And to whute whutes three.

That will I doe, said Robin Hood,
  Or else I were to blame;
Three whutes in a fryer's fist
  Would make me glad and faine.

The fryer set his fist to his mouth,
  And whuted whutes three:
Half a hundred good band-dogs
  Came running over the lee.

"Here is for every man a dog,
  And I myselfe for thee."
Nay, by my faith, said Robin Hood,
  Fryer, that may not be.

Two dogs at once to Robin Hood did goe,
  The one behind, the other before,
Robin Hood's mantle of Lincolne greene
  Off from his backe they tore.

And whether his men shot east or west,
  Or they shot north or south,
The curtall dogs, so taught they were,
  They caught th' arrows in their mouth.

Take up thy dogs, said Little John,
  Fryer, at my bidding be.
Whose man art thou, said the curtall fryer,
  Comes here to prate with me?

"I am Little John, Robin Hood's man,
  Fryer, I will not lie;
If thou take not up thy dogs soone,
  I'le take up them and thee."

Little John had a bow in his hand,
  He shot with might and main;
Soon halfe a score of the fryer's dogs
  Lay dead upon the plain.

Hold thy hand, good fellow, said the curtal fryer,
  Thy master and I will agree;
And we will have new orders taken,
  With all hast that may be.

"If thou wilt forsake fair Fountaine's dale,
  And Fountaine's Abbey free,
Every Sunday throwout the yeere,
  A noble shall be thy fee:

And every holiday through the yeere,
  Changed shall thy garment be,
If thou wilt goe to faire Nottingham,
  And there remaine with me."

This curtal fryer had kept Fountaine's Dale
  Seven long yeeres and more,
There was neither knight, lord, nor carle,
  Could make him yeeld before.

Fountain's Abbey.—P. 180.

THE NOBLE FISHER-MAN;
OR, ROBIN HOOD'S PREFERMENT:

SHOWING how he won a prize on the sea, and how he gave one halfe to his dame, and the other to the building of almes-houses. The tune is, In summer time, etc.

From three old black-letter copies; one in the Collection of Anthony à Wood, another in the British Museum, and the third in a private Collection. This is one of the ballads contained in Mr. Peck's MS. alluded to in the Editor's preface, vol. i. p. xxvii. etc. Mr. Peck has rendered it into more modern language and added three or four stanzas; but has certainly not improved the version. He calls it a piscatory song, and entitles it " Simon over the Lee."

In summer time, when leaves grow green,
　　When they doe grow both green and long,—
Of a bold outlaw, call'd Robin Hood,
　　It is of him I do sing this song,—
When the lilly leaf, and the eglantine,*
　　Doth bud and spring with a merry cheere,
This outlaw was weary of the wood side,
　　And chasing of the fallow deere.

* In the first edition of Ritson the word "elephant" is used; which is evidently a corruption. In two early copies with which the Editor has compared this ballad, he finds "eglantine" and "cowslip sweet" substituted; both preferable, and he has chosen eglantine.

"The fisher-men brave more mony have
  Than any merchants two or three;
Therefore I will to Scarborough go,
  That I a fisherman brave may be."

This outlaw called his merry men all,
  As they sate under the green-wood tree :
"If any of you have gold to spend,
  I pray you heartily spend it with me."

Now, quoth Robin Hood, Ile to Scarborough go,
  It seems to be a very faire day.
He took up his inne at a widdow woman's house,
  Hard by upon the water gray :

Who asked of him, where wert thon borne?
  Or tell to me where dost thou fare ?
I am a poor fisherman, said he then,
  This day intrapped all in care.

"What is thy name, thou fine fellow,
  I pray thee heartily tell it to me ?"
"In my own country, where I was borne,
  Men call me Simon over the Lee."

Simon, Simon, said the good wife,
  I wish thou mayest well brook* thy name.
The out-law was ware of her courtesie,
  And rejoyced he had got such a dame.

"Simon, wilt thou be my man ?
  And good round wages Ile give thee;
I have as good a ship of my own,
  As any sails upon the sea.

---

* "I wish thou mayest well brook thy name." On this
line Mr. Peck subjoins the following note :—"Mayst thou
be as fortunate, and prove as good a fisherman as thy
name-sake, Simon Peter. She wishes thus for her own
sake, intending to hire him."

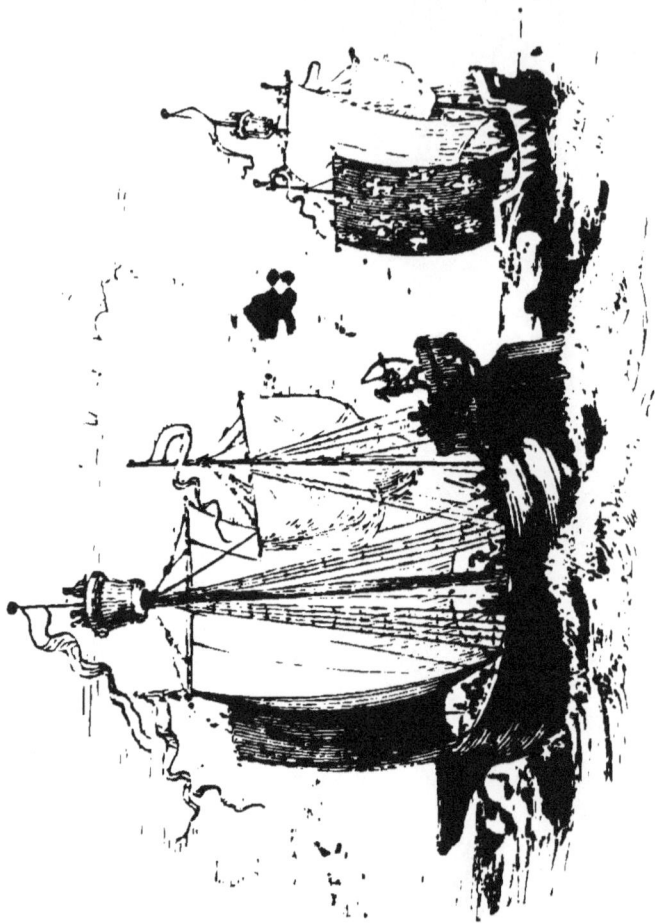

The Noble Fisher-man.—P. 183.

Anchors and planks thou shalt not want,
Masts and ropes that are so long."
And if you thus do furnish me,
Said Simon, nothing shall goe wrong.

They pluckt up anchor, and away did sayle,
More of a day than two or three;
When others cast in their baited hooks,
The bare lines into the sea cast he.

It will be long, said the master then,
Ere this great lubber do thrive on the sea;
I'le assure you he shall have no share of our fish,
For in truth he is no part worthy.

O woe is me! said Simon then,
This day that ever I came here!
I wish I were in Plompton parke,
In chasing of the fallow deere.

For every clowne laughs me to scorne,
And by me sets nothing at all;
If I had them in Plompton park,
I would set as little by them all.

They pluckt up anchor, and away did sayle,
More of a day than two or three:
But Simon espyed a ship of warre,
That sayled towards them most valorously.

O woe is me! said the master then,
This day that ever I was borne!
For all our fish we have got to-day,
Is every bit lost and forlorne.

For your French robbers on the sea.
They will not spare of us one man,
But carry us to the coast of France,
And lay us in the prison strong.

But Simon said, doe not feare them,
  Neither, master, take you no care;
Give me my bent bow in my hand,
  And never a Frenchman will I spare.

" Hold thy peace, thou long lubbèr,
  For thou art nought but brags and boast;
If I should cast thee over-board,
  There's but a simple lubber lost."

Simon grew angry at these words,
  And so angry then was he,
That he took his bent bow in his hand,
  And in the ship-hatch goeth he.

Master, tye me to the mast, saith he,
  That at my mark I may stand fair,
And give me my bent bow in my hand,
  And never a Frenchman will I spare.

He drew his arrow to the head,
  And drewe it with all his might and maine,
And straightway, in the twinkling of an eye,
  To the Frenchman's heart the arrow's gane.

The Frenchman fell down on the ship hatch,
  And under the hatches down below;
Another Frenchman, that him espy'd,
  The dead corpse into the sea doth throw.

O master, loose me from the mast, he said,
  And for them all take you no care;
For give me my bent bow in my hand,
  And never a Frenchman will I spare.

Then streight they boarded the French ship,
  They lyeing all dead in their sight;
They found within that ship of warre,
  Twelve thousand pound of mony bright.

The one halfe of the ship, said Simon then,
  Ile give to my dame and her children small;
The other halfe of the ship Ile bestow
  On you that are my fellowes all.

But now bespake the master then,
  For so, Simon, it shall not be,
For you have won it with your own hand,
  And the owner of it you shall bee.

"It shall be so, as I have said;
  And, with this gold, for the opprest
An habitation I will build,
  Where they shall live in peace and rest."

What's in thy bag, and bottle; I say,
  Come tell it unto me.

"What's that to thee? thou proud fellow,
  Tell me as I do stand;
What hast thou to do with my bag and bottle?
  Let me see thy command."

"My sword, which hangeth by my side,
  Is my command I know;
Come, let me taste of thy bottle,
  Or it may breed thy woe."

"The devil a drop, thou proud fellow,
  Of my bottle thou shalt see,
Until thy valour here be tried,
  Whether thou wilt fight or flee."

What shall we fight for? cries Robin Hood,
  Come tell it unto me;
Here is twenty pound in good red gold,
  Win it, and take it thee.

The shepherd stood all in amaze,
  And knew not what to say:
"I have no money, thou proud fellow,
  But bag and bottle I'll lay."

"I am content, thou shepherd swain,
  Fling them down on the ground;
But it will breed thee mickle pain,
  To win my twenty pound."

"Come draw thy sword, thou proud fellow,
  Thou standest too long to prate;
This hook of mine shall let thee know,
  A coward I do hate.'

So they fell to it, full hard and sore,
    It was on a summer's day,
From ten till four in the afternoon
    The shepherd held him play.

Robin's buckler proved his chief'st defence,
    And saved him many a bang,
For every blow the shepherd gave
    Made Robin's sword cry twang.

Many a sturdie blow the shepherd gave,
    And that bold Robin found,
Till the blood ran trickling from his head,
    Then he fell to the ground.

"Arise, arise, thou proud fellow,
    And thou shalt have fair play,
If thou wilt yield, before thou go,
    That I have won the day."

A boon, a boon, cry'd bold Robin,
    If that a man thou be,
Then let me take my beugle horn,
    And blow out blasts three.

Then said the shepherd to bold Robin,
    To that I will agree;
For if thou shouldst blow till to-morrow morn,
    I scorn one foot to flee.

Then Robin he set his horn to his mouth,
    And he blew with might and main,
Until he espied Little John
    Come tripping over the plain.

"O who is yonder, thou proud fellow,
    That comes down yonder hill?"
"Yonder is John, bold Robin Hood's man,
    Shall fight with thee thy fill."

What is the matter? said Little John,
    Master, come tell unto me.
My case is bad, cries Robin Hood,
    For the shepherd hath conquer'd me.

I am glad of that, cries Little John:
    Shepherd, turn thou to me;
For a bout with thee I mean to have,
    Either come fight or flee.

"With all my heart, thou proud fellow,
    For it never shall be said
That a shepherd's hook at thy sturdy look
    Will one jot be dismaied."

So they fell to it, full hard and sore,
    Striving for victorie.
I will know, says John, ere we give o'er,
    Whether thou wilt fight or flee.

The shepherd gave John a sturdie blow,
    With his hook under the chin.
Beshrew thy heart, said Little John,
    Thou basely dost begin.

Nay, that is nothing, said the shepherd,
    Either yield to me the daie,
Or I will bang thy back and sides,
    Before thou goest thy way.

What, dost thou think, thou proud fellow,
    That thou canst conquer me?
Nay, thou shalt know, before thou go,
    I'll fight before I'll flee.

Again the shepherd laid on him,
    Just as he first begun.
Hold thy hand, cry'd bold Robin,
    I will yield the wager won.

With all my heart, said Little John,
   To that I will agree;
For he is the flower of shepherd swains,
   The like I did never see.

Thus have you heard of Robin Hood,
   Also of Little John;
How a shepherd swain did conquer them;
   The like was never known.

Robin Hood's Golden Prize.—P. 191.

ROBIN HOOD'S GOLDEN PRIZE.

" He met two priests upon the way,
   And forced them with him to pray;
   For gold they prayed, and gold they had,
   Enough to make bold Robin glad!
   His share came to four hundred pound,
   That then was told upon the ground.
   Now mark, and you shall hear the jest,
   You never heard the like exprest.

Tune is, Robin Hood was a tall young man, &c."

This ballad (given from an old black-letter copy in the
Collection of Anthony à Wood) was entered, amongst
others, in the Stationers' book, by Francis Coule, 13th
June, 1631; and by Francis Grove, 2d June, 1656.
Compared with the copy in the Roxburgh Collection

I HAVE heard talk of bold Robin Hood,
     Derry, derry down,
  And of brave Little John,
Of fryer Tuck, and William Scarlet,
  Loxley, and maid Marion.

But such a tale as this before
  I think there was never none;
For Robin Hood disguised himself,
  And to the green wood is gone.

Like to a fryer bold Robin Hood
  Was accoutred in his array;
With hood, gown, beads, and crucifix,
  He past upon the way.

He had not gone miles two or three,
    But it was his chance to spy
Two lusty priests, clad all in black,
    Come riding gallantly.

Benedicite, then said Robin Hood,
    Some pitty on me take ;
Cross you my hand with a silver groat,
    For our dear ladie's sake.

For I have been wand'ring all this day,
    And nothing could I get ;
Not so much as one poor cup of drink,
    Nor bit of bread to eat.

Now, by our holy dame,* the priests reply'd,
    We never a penny have ;
For we this morning have been robb'd,
    And could no money save.

I am afraid, said Robin Hood,
    That you both do tell a lie ;
And now before you do go hence,
    I am resolv'd to try.

When as the priests heard him say so,
    Then they rode away amain ;
But Robin Hood took to his heels,
    And soon overtook them again.

Then Robin Hood laid hold of them both,
    And pull'd them down from their horse :
O spare us, fryer ! the priests cry'd out,
    On us have some remorse !

---

* *Our holy dame.* The virgin Mary (so called); unless, for " *our holy dame,*" we should read *our halidome*, which may mean our holyness, honesty, chastity : *haligdome, sanctimonia,* " Lye's Saxon Dictionary."

You said you had no money, quoth he,
    Wherefore, without delay,
We three will fall down on our knees,
    And for money we will pray.

The priests they could not him gainsay,
    But down they kneel'd with speed :
Send us, O send us, then quoth they,
    Some money to serve our need.

The priests did pray with a mournful cheer,
    Sometimes their hands did wring ;
Sometimes they wept, and cried aloud,
    Whilst Robin did merrily sing.

When they had been praying an hour's space,
    The priests did still lament ;
Then quoth bold Robin, now let us see
    What money heaven hath sent.

We will now be sharers all alike
    Of the money that we have ;
And there is never a one of us
    That his fellow shall deceive.

The priests their hands in their pockets put,
    But money could find none :
We'll search ourselves, said Robin Hood,
    Each other, one by one.

Then Robin took pains to search them both,
    And he found good store of gold,
Five hundred peices presently
    Upon the grass was told.

Here is a brave show, said Robin Hood,
    Such store of gold to see,
And you shall each one have a part,
    Cause you pray'd so heartily.

He gave them fifty pounds a-peice,
   And the rest for himself did keep:
The priests durst not speak one word,
   But they sighed wondrous deep.

With that the priests rose up from their knees,
   Thinking to have parted so :
Nay, stay, says Robin Hood, one thing more
   I have to say ere you do go.

You shall be sworn, said bold Robin Hood,
   Upon this holy grass,
That you will never tell lies again,
   Which way soever you pass.

The second oath that you here must take, .
   That all the days of your lives,
You shall never tempt maids to sin,
   Nor lye with other men's wives.

The last oath you shall take, is this,
   Be charitable to the poor ;
Say, you have met with a holy fryar,
   And I desire no more.

He set them on their horses again,
   And away they then did ride ;
And he return'd to the merry green-wood,
   With great joy, mirth, and pride.
      Hey down, derry down.

ROBIN HOOD'S CHASE:

Or, a merry progress between Robin Hood and King Henry. Shewing how Robin Hood led the king his chase from London to London; and when he had taken his leave of the queen, he returned to merry Sherwood. To the tune of Robin Hood and the Beggar.

From an old black-letter copy in the Collection of Anthony à Wood, compared with the Roxburgh copy.

Come, you gallants all, to you I do call,
        With hey down, down, an a down,
  That now are in this place;
For a song I will sing of Henry the king,
  How he did Robin Hood chase.

Queen Katherine she a match did make,
  As plainly doth appear,
For three hundred tun of good red wine,
  And three hundred tun of beere.

But yet her archers she had to seek,
  With their bows and arrows so good;
But her mind it was bent with a good intent,
  To send for bold Robin Hood.

But when bold Robin he came there,
  Queen Katherine she did say,
Thou art welcome, Locksley, said the queen,
  And all thy yeomen gay.

For a match of shooting I have made,
    And thou on my part, Robin, must be.
"If I miss the mark, be it light or dark,
    Then hanged I will be."

But when the game came to be play'd,
    Bold Robin then drew nigh,
With his mantle of green, most brave to be seen,
    He let his arrows fly.

And when the game it ended was,
    Bold Robin won it with a grace ;
But after the king was angry with him,
    And vow'd he would him chace.

What though his pardon granted was,
    While he with him did stay ;
Yet after the king was vex'd at him,
    When he was gone his way.

Soon after the king from the court did hye,
    In a furious angry mood,
And did often enquire both far and near
    After bold Robin Hood.

And when the king to Nottingham came,
    Bold Robin was in the wood :
O, come now, said he, and let me see
    Who can find me bold Robin Hood.

But when that bold Robin he did hear
    The king had him in chase,
Then said Little John, 'tis time to be gone,
    And go to some other place.

Then away they went from merry Sherwood,
    And into Yorkshire did hye ;
And the king did follow, with a whoop and a hallo,
    But could not come him nigh.

Yet jolly Robin he passed along,
    He went to Newcastle town ;
And there stayed he hours two or three,
    For he then to Barwick was gone.

When the king did see how Robin did flee,
    He was vexed wondrous sore ;
With a whoop and a hallo he vow'd him to follow,
    And take him, or never give o'er.

Come now let's away, then cries Little John,
    Let any man follow that dare ;
To Carlisle we'll hie, with our company,
    And so then to Lancastèr.

From Lancaster then to Chester they went,
    And so did king Henry ;
But Robin went away, for he durst not stay,
    For fear of some treachery.

Says Robin, let us for London go,
    To see our noble queen's face,
It may be she wants our company,
    Which makes the king so us chase.

When Robin he came queene Katherine before,
    He fell low upon his knee :
"If it please your grace, I am come to this place
    For to speak with king Henry."

Queen Katherine answered bold Robin again,
    The king is gone to merry Sherwood :
When he went away, to me he did say,
    He would go seek Robin Hood.

" Then fare you well, my gracious queen,
    For to Sherwood I will hye apace ;
For fain would I see what he would with me,
    If I could but meet with his grace."

When as king Henry he came home,
  Full weary, and vexed in mind,
And that he did hear, Robin had been there,
  He blamed dame Fortune unkind.

You're welcome home, queen Katherine cryed,
  Henry, my soveraign liege;
Bold Robin Hood, that archer good,
  Your person hath been to seek.

But when king Henry did hear,
  That Robin had been him to seek,
This answer he gave, He's a cunning knave,
  For I have sought him this whole three week

A boon! a boon! queen Katherine cry'd,
  I beg it here of your grace,
To pardon his life, and seek no more strife:
  And so endeth Robin Hood's chase.

Little John and the Four Beggars.—P. 199.

LITTLE JOHN AND THE FOUR BEGGARS.

From an old black-letter copy in the Collection of Anthony
à Wood : the full title being, "A new merry song of Robin
Hood and Little John, showing how Little John went a
begging, and how he fought with the four baggers. The
tune is Robin Hood and the Beggar:" compared, by the
editor, with the Roxburgh copy, which has for its head
piece, a Beggar leading a Dog.

ALL you that delight to spend some time,
    With a hey down, down, a down, down,
  A merry song for to sing,
Unto me draw near, and you shall hear
  How Little John went a begging.

As Robin Hood walked the forest along,
  And all his yeomandree,
Says Robin, some of you must a begging go, *
  And, Little John, it must be thee.

Sayes John, if I must a begging go,
  I will have a palmer's weed,
With a staff and a coat, and bags of all sort,
  The better then I shall speed.

  * It is not at all improbable, but that as high as Robin
Hood and his men carried it, they were now and then
put to their shifts, and sometimes forced to beg in good
earnest.—*Peck's MSS.*

Come, give me now a bag for my bread,
  And another for my cheese,
And one for a penny, when I get any,
  That nothing I may leese.

Now Little John is a begging gone,
  Seeking for some relief;
But of all the beggars he met on the way,
  Little John he was the chief.

But as he was walking himself alone,
  Four beggars he chanced to spy,
Some deaf, and some blind, and some came behind;
  Says John, here's brave company.

Good-morrow, said John, my brethren dear,
  Good fortune I had you to see;
Which way do you go? pray let me know,
  For I want some company.

O! what is here to do? then said Little John:
  Why ring all these bells? said he;
What dog is a hanging? come, let us be ganging,
  That we the truth may see.

Here is no dog a hanging, then one of them said,
  Good fellow, we tell unto thee;
But here is one dead, will give us cheese and bread,
  And it may be one single penny.*

* It was the custom in popish times to give bread and
money to all manner of persons, without distinction, who
came to assist at the funeral of a deceased neighbour; and
this in order to engage them to pray the more heartily
for the soul of the defunct. And it is yet usual among
those of a lower or middle rank in the north parts of
England, to send the baker, when any of the family dies,
in their names, to distribute at every house in the parish,
as many penny loaves as there are persons, men, women,
and children, in each family; likewise generally a small

We have brethren in London, another he said,
  So have we in Coventry,
In Barwick and Dover, and all the world over,
  But ne'er a crookt carril* like thee.

Therefore stand thou back, thou crooked carèl,
  And take that knock on the crown.
Nay, said Little John, Ile not be gone,
  For a bout will I have with you round.

Now have at you all, then said Little John,
  If you be so full of your blows;
Fight on all four, and nere give o'er,
  Whether you be friends or foes.

John nipped the dumb, and made him to rore;
  And the blind that he could not see,
And he that a cripple had been seven years,
  He made run faster than he.

And flinging them all against the wall,
  With many a sturdie bang,
It made John sing, to hear the gold ring,
  Which against the walls cryed twang.

Then he got out of the beggar's cloak
  Three hundred pound in gold ;
Good fortune had I, then said Little John,
  Such a good sight to behold.

plumb-cake. Rich men's fune als are now otherwise
managed. There is an abundance of persons on horse, a
crowd of coaches and pretended mourners, a deal of pomp
and pageantry almost without end : all which does neither
the poor nor themselves any good at all; but rarely any
dole, in which I think (though I am no papist), the money
were far better bestowed. The word dole is derived from
the Dutch, *daylen*—minister. Whence the English to deal
or give out a thing.—*Peck*.
  * Carl. old fellow.

But what found he in a beggar's bag
  But three hundred pound and three ?
" If I drink water while this doth last,
  Then an evil death may I dye. *

* There is an old book called "The tunning of Elynor
Rummin, the famous ale-wife of England, by John
Skelton," two sheets and a half, 4to. London, 1624. In
the title-page is the picture of an old ill-favored woman
holding in her hand a black pot of ale, and underneath
these verses :—

  " When Skelton wore the laurel crown,
  My ale put all the ale-wifes down."
                    Ath. Oxon. vol. i. p. 23.

I have not seen the book of Elynor Rummin's, but a
friend tells me, it is only a merry tale of some jovial
gossips got together and pawning all they could rap and
rend, to purchase her good ale, near Guildford, in Surrey.
These good women remind me of the proverb, "Gossips
and Frogs may drink and talk." Robin Hood and his men
were much of the same temper with these tattling gossips :
for whatever they could lay their hands on, it was presently
turned into good liquor, and away it went, as the old song
says, "Merrily down the red lane." Peggy Dowker, of
Chesterfield, was of late years as famous for good ale as
Elynor Rummin. I cannot help thinking, but the learned
Dr. King had her in his eye, when he wrote his instructions
how to brew and bottle :—

  " Oh ! Peggy, Peggy, when thou goest to brew,
  Consider well what you're about to do ;
  Be very wise, very sedately think,
  That what you're going now to make is *drink;*
  Consider who must drink that drink, and then,
  What 'tis to have the praise of *honest* men ;
  For surely, Peggy, while that drink does last,
  'Tis Peggy will be *toasted* or *disgrac'd.*
  Then, if thy ale in *glass* thou would'st confine,
  To make its sparkling rays in beauty shine,
  Let thy clean bottle be entirely dry,
  Lest a white substance to the surface fly,
  And, floating there, disturb the curious eye.

And my begging trade I will now give o'er,
　My fortune it hath bin so good ;
Therefore Ile not stay, but I will away,
　To the forrest of merry Sherwood."

And when to the forrest of Sherwood he came,
　He quickly there did see
His master good, bold Robin Hood,
　And all his company.

What news? What news? then said Robin Hood,
　Come, Little John, tell unto me ;
How hast thou sped with thy beggar's trade ?
　For that I fain would see.

No news but good, said Little John,
　With begging full well I have sped ;
Six hundred and three I have here for thee,
　In silver and gold so red.

Then Robin took Little John by the hand,
　And danced about the oak tree :
" If we drink water while this doth last,
　Then an ill death may we die."

So to conclude my merry new song,
　All you that delight it to sing ;
'Tis of Robin Hood, that archer good,
　And how Little John went a begging.

　　　But this great maxim must be understood,
　　　' Be sure, nay very sure, thy *cork* be good !'
　　　Then future ages shall of Peggy tell,
　　　That nymph that *brew'd* and *bottled* ale so wel.
　　　　Bishop King's works, Mully of Mountown.

　　　　　　　　　　　　—*Peck's MSS.*

ROBIN HOOD'S DELIGHT:

OR, a merry combat fought between Robin Hood, Little John, and Will Scarelock, and three stout keepers in Sheerwood Forrest.

> " Robin was valiant and stout,
>   So was Scarelock and John in the field,
> But these keepers stout did give them rout,
>   And make them all for to yield.
> But after the battel ended was,
>   Bold Robin did make them amends,
> For claret and sack they did not lack,
>   So drank themselves good friends."

To the tune of Robin Hood and Queen Katherine; or, Robin Hood and the Shepherd.—*Ritson.*

Dr. Pepusch, among other very curious articles of ancient English music, was possessed of a MS. folio (supposed to be still extant), which, at p. 15, contained a tune entitled "Robin Hood." See Ward's "Lives of the Professors of Gresham College," 1740, (an interleaved copy, corrected and augmented by the author, in the British Museum). "Robene Hude" is likewise the name of a dance in Wedderburn's "Complainte of Scotland," printed in 1549. The tune is preserved by Oswald, in his "Caledonian Pocket Companion."

From an old black-letter copy in the Collection of Anthony à Wood.

THERE's some will talk of lords and knights,
    Doun, a doun, a doun,
And some of yeomen good ;
But I will tell you of Will Scarlock,
    Little John, and Robin Hood.
        Doun, a doun, a doun, a doun.

They were outlaws, 'tis well known,
  And men of a noble blood;
And many a time was their valour shown
  In the forest of merry Sheerwood.

Upon a time it chanced so,
  As Robin would have it be,
They all three would a walking go,
  The pastime for to see.

And as they walked the forest along,
  Upon a Midsummer day,
There were they aware of three keepèrs,
  Clad all in green aray.

With brave long faucheons by their sides,
  And forrest-bills in hand,
They call'd aloud to those bold outlàws,
  And charged them to stand.

Why, who are you, cry'd bold Robin,
  That speak so boldly here?
" We three belong to King Henry,
  And are keepers of his deer."

The devil you are ! sayes Robin Hood,
  I am sure that it is not so ;
We be the keepers of this forrèst,
  And that you soon shall know.

Come, your coats of green lay on the ground,
  And so will we all three,
And take your swords and bucklers round,
  And try the victory.

We be content, the keepers said,
  We be three, and you no less,
Then why should we be of you afraid,
  As we never did transgress ?

" Why, if you be three keepers in this forrèst,
    Then we be three rangers good,
And will make you know before you do go,
    You meet with bold Robin Hood."

" We be content, thou bold outlàw,
    Our valour here to try,
And will make you know, before we do go,
    We will fight before we will fly.

Then, come draw your swords, you bold outlàws,
    No longer stand to prate,
But let us try it out with blows,
    For cowards we do hate.

Here is one of us for Will Scarlock,
    And another for Little John,
And I myself for Robin Hood,
    Because he is stout and strong."

So they fell to it hard and sore,
    It was on a Midsummer's day ;
From eight of the clock till two and past,
    They all shewed gallant play.

There Robin, and Will, and Little John,
    They fought most manfully,
Till all their winde was spent and gone,
    Then Robin aloud did cry :

O hold, O hold, cries bold Robin,
    I see you be stout men ;
Let me blow one blast on my bugle horn,
    Then Ile fight with you again.

" That bargain's to make, bold Robin Hood,
    Therefore we it deny ;
Thy blast upon the bugle horn
    Cannot make us fight or fly.

Therefore fall on, or else be gone,
    And yield to us the day :
It never shall be said that we are afraid
    Of thee, nor thy yeomen gay."

If that be so, cries bold Robin,
    Let me but know your names,
And in the forrest of merry Sheerwood,
    I shall extol your fames.

And with our names, one of them said,
    What hast thou here to do ?
Except that thou wilt fight it out,
    Our names thou shalt not know.

We will fight no more, sayes bold Robin,
    You be men of valour stout ;
Come and go with me to Nottingham,
    And there we will fight it out.

With a but of sack we will bang it about,
    To see who wins the day ;
And for the cost make you no doubt,
    I have gold enough to pay.

And ever hereafter so long as we live,
    We all will brethren be ;
For I love these men with heart and hand,
    That will fight and never flee.

So, away they went to Nottingham,
    With sack to make amends ;
For three days they the wine did chase,
    And drank themselves good friends.

ROBIN HOOD AND THE BEGGAR.

IN TWO PARTS.

MR. RITSON considers this ballad to be a Scottish com-
position of some antiquity, and states that he gives it
from a modern copy printed at Newcastle, where "he
accidentally picked it up." Robin Hood was doubtless a
popular hero with Scottish, as well as English minstrels;
and Mr. Gutch confirms the conjecture by printing the
ballad from a copy evidently unknown to Mr. Ritson, in
Wood's study, in the Ashmolean Museum, bearing the
imprint of A. Keith, Aberdeen. This latter copy restores
some lines which are wanting in Ritson's edition, and
includes several important corrections.

LYTH and listen, gentlemen,
    That's come of high born blood,
I'll tell you of a brave booting
    That befel Robin Hood.

Robin Hood upon a day,
    He went forth alone,
And as he came from Barnesdale
    Into fair evening,

He met a beggar on the way,
    Who sturdily could gang;
He had a pike-staff in his hand
    That was baith stark and strang;

Robin Hood and the Beggar.—P. 208.

A clouted cloak about him was,
    That held him frae the cold,
The thinnest bit of it, I guess,
    Was more than twenty fold.

His meal-pock haug about his neck,
    Into a leathern fang,
Well fasten'd with a broad buckle,
    That was baith stark and strang.

He had three hats upon his head,
    Together stickèd fast,
He car'd neither for wind nor weet,
    In lands where'er he past.

Good Robin coost him in his way,
    To see what he might be,
If any beggar had monèy,
    He thought some part had he.

Tarry, tarry, good Robin says,
    Tarry, and speak with me.
He heard him as he heard him not,
    And fast on his way can hie.

It be's not so, says good Robin,
    Nay, thou must tarry still.
By my troth, said the bold beggàr,
    Of that I have no will.

It is far to my lodging house,
    And it is growing late,
If they have supt e'er I come in
    I will look wondrous blate.*

Now, by my truth, says good Robin,
    I see well by thy fare,

* Sheepish, or foolish, as we should now say.

P

If thou chear well to thy suppèr,
  Of mine thou takes no care,
Who wants my dinner all this day,
  And wots not where to lie,
And should I to the tavern go,
  I want monèy to buy.

Sir, thou must lend me some monèy
  Till we two meet again.
The beggar answer'd cankerdly,
  I have no money to lend :

Thou art as young a man as I,
  And seems to be as sweir ; *
If thou fast till thou get from me,
  Thou shalt eat none this year.

Now, by my truth, says good Robìn,
  Since we are 'sembled so,
If thou have but a small farthing,
  I'll have it e'er thou go.

Therefore, lay down thy clouted cloak,
  And do no longer stand,
And loose the strings of all thy pocks,
  I'll ripe them with my hand.

And now to thee I make a vow,
  If thou make any din,
I shall see if a broad arròw,
  Can pierce a beggar's skin.

The beggar smil'd, and answer made,
  Far better let me be ;
Think not that I will be afraid,
  For thy nip † crooked tree ,

---

* Lazy, indolent.
† *Nip* (in Scotch), paring, shred, little bit: *q. l.* you
paltry bit of a stick or bird-bolt.

Or that I fear thee any whit,
  For thy curn* up of sticks,
I know no use for them so meet
  As to be pudding-pricks.†

Here I defy thee to do me ill,
  For all thy boisterous fare,
Thou'st get nothing from me but ill,
  Would'st thou seek evermair.

Good Robin bent his noble bow,
  He was an angry man,
And in it set a broad arrow;
  Yet erst‡ was drawn a span,

The beggar, with his noble tree,
  Reach'd him so round a rout,
That his bow and his broad arrow
  In flinders§ flew about.

Good Robin bound‖ him to his brand,
  But that prov'd likewise vain,
The beggar lighted on his hand
  With his pike-staff again:

I wot he might not draw a sword
  For forty days and mair.
Good Robin could not speak a word,
  His heart was never so sair.

He could not fight, he could not flee,
  He wist not what to do;
The beggar with his noble tree
  Laid lusty flaps him to.

* An indefinite quantity.—*Scotticism.*
† Skewers that fasten the pudding-bag.
‡ Before.
§ Splinters.
‖ Betook.

He paid good Robin back and side,
　And beft him up and down,
And with his pike-staff still laid on hard,
　Till he fell in a swoon.

Fy, stand up, man, the beggar said,
　'Tis shame to go to rest ;
Stay still, till thou get my monèy,
　I think it were the best :

And syne go to the tavern house,
　And buy both wine and ale ;
Hereat thy friends will crack full crouse,
　Thou hast been at a dale.

Good Robin answer'd never a word,
　But lay still as a stane ;
His cheeks were white as any clay,
　And closed were his eyen.

The beggar thought him dead but fail,
　And boldly bown'd away.—
I would you had been at the dale,
　And gotten part of the play.

————————

[THE SECOND PART.]

Now three of Robin's men, by chance,
　Came walking by the way,
And found their master in a trance,
　On ground where he did lay.

Up have they taken good Robin,
　Making a piteous beir,*

* Noise.

Yet saw they no man there at whom
  They might the matter speir.
They lookèd him all round about,
  But wounds on him saw none,
Yet at his mouth came bocking out*
  The blood of a good vein.

Cold water they have taken syne,
  And cast into his face ;
Then he began to lift his eyne,
  And spake within short space ;

Tell us, dear master, said his men,
  How with you stands the case ?
Good Robin sigh'd e'er he began
  To tell of his disgrace.

"I have been watchman in this wood
  Near hand this forty year,
Yet I was never so hard bestead
  As you have found me here ;

A beggar with a clouted cloak,
  In whom I fear'd no ill,
Hath with his pike-staff claw'd my back,
  I fear 'twill ne'er be well.

See, where he goes o'er yonder hill,
  With hat upon his head ;
If e'er you lov'd your master well,
  Go now revenge this deed ;

And bring him back again to me,
  If it lie in your might,
That I may see, before I die,
  Him punisht in my sight :

* *Bock*—vomit.

And if you may not bring him back,
  Let him not go loose on ;
For to us all it were great shame
  If he escap't again."

"One of us shall with you remain,
  Because you're ill at ease,
The other two shall bring him back,
  To use him as you please."

Now, by my troth, says good Robin,
  I trow there's enough said ;
If he get scouth* to wield his tree,
  I fear you'll both be paid.

"Be ye not fear'd, our good master,
  That we two can be dung†
With any blutter‡ base beggar,
  That has nought but a rung.

His staff shall stand him in no stead,
  That you shall shortly see,
But back again he shall be led,
  And fast bound shall he be,
To see if ye will have him slain,
  Or hangèd on a tree."

"But cast you slily in his way,
  Before he be aware,
And on his pike-staff first hands lay,
  You'll speed the better far."

Now leave we Robin with his man,
  Again to play the child,

* Liberty.
† Beaten, overcome.
‡ *Bluter.* Mr. Ritson queries the meaning of this word.
It is blutter, a rumbling noise.—*Jameson.*

And learn himself to stand and gang
   By haulds,* for all his eild.†

Now pass we to the bold beggàr,
   That rakèd ‡ o'er the hill,
Who never mended his pace no more,
   Nor he had done no ill.

The young men knew the country well,
   So soon where he would be,§
And they have taken another way,
   Was nearer by miles three.

They rudely ran with all their might,
   Spared neither dub nor mire,
They started neither at laigh nor hight,
   No travel made them tire,

Till they before the beggar wan,
   And coost them in his way ;
A little wood lay in a glen,
   And there they both did stay ;

They stood up closely by a tree,
   In ilk ‖ side of the gate,
Until the beggar came them to,
   That thought not of such fate :

And as he was betwixt them past,
   They leapt upon him baith ;
The one his pike-staff grippèd fast,
   They fearèd for its scaith.

---

* Holds, holding places, supports.
† Age.
‡ Walked apace.
§ Wanting in the original, and restored from the Aberdeen copy.
‖ Each.

The other he held in his sight
  A drawn dirk to his breast,
And said, false carl, quit thy staff,
  Or I shall be thy priest.

His pike-staff they have taken him frae,
  And stuck it in the green,
He was full loath to let it gae,
  If better might have been.

The beggar was the fear'dest man
  Of one that ever might be,
To win away no way he can,
  Nor help him with his tree.

He wist not wherefore he was tane,
  Nor how many was there ;
He thought his life days had been gane,
  He grew into despair ;

Grant me my life, the beggar said,
  For him that died on tree,
And take away that ugly knife,
  Or then for fear I'll die.

I griev'd you never in all my life,
  Nor late nor yet by ayre,
Ye have great sin, if ye would slay
  A silly poor beggar.

Thou lies, false lown, they said again,
  By all that may be sworn ;
Thou hast near slain the gentlest man
  That ever yet was born ;

And back again thou shalt be led,
  And fast bound shalt thou be,
To see if he will have thee slain
  Or hangèd on a tree.

The beggar then thought all was wrong,
  They were set for his wrack,
He saw nothing appearing then,
  But ill upon worse back.

Were he out of their hands, he thought,
  And had again his tree,
He should not be had back for nought,
  With such as he did see.

Then he bethought him on a wile,
  If it could take effect,
How he the young men might beguile,
  And give them a begeck.

Thus for to do them shame or ill,
  His beastly breast was bent,
He found the wind grew something shril,
  To further his intent.

He said, Brave gentlemen, be good,
  And let the poor man be ;
When ye have taken a beggar's blood,
  It helps you not a flea.

It was but in my own defence,
  If he hath gotten skaith ;
But I will make a recompense,
  Much better for you baith.

If ye will set me safe and free,
  And do me no dangèr,
An hundred pounds I will you give,
  And much more good silvèr,

That I have gather'd this many years,
  Under this clouted cloak,
And hid up privately,
  In bottom of my pock.

The young men to a council yeed,
   And let the beggar gae ;
They wist full well he had no speed
   From them to run away.

They thought they would the money take,
   Come after what so may ;
And then they would not bring him back,
   But in that place him slay.

By that good Robin would not know
   That they had gotten coin,
It would content him for to show
   That there they had him slain.

They said, False carl, soon have done,
   And tell forth thy monèy,
For the ill turn that thou hast done
   'Tis but a simple fee ;

And yet we will not have thee back,
   Come after what so may,
If thou will do that which thou spake,
   And make us present pay.

O then he loos'd his clouted cloak,
   And spread it on the ground,
And thereon laid he many a pock,
   Betwixt them and the wind.

He took a great bag from his hase,
   It was near full of meal,
Two pecks in it at least there was,
   And more I wot full well.

Upon his cloak he laid it down,
   The mouth he open'd wide,
To turn the same he made him bown,
   The young men ready spy'd ;

In every hand he took a nook
  Of that great leathern meal,
And with a fling the meal he shook
  Into their faces hail :

Wherewith he blinded them so close,
  A stime they could not see ;
And then in heart he did rejoice,
  And clapt his lusty tree.

He thought if he had done them wrong,
  In mealing of their cloaths,
For to strick off the meal again
  With his pike-staff he goes.

Or any of them could red their eyne,
  Or could a glimm'ring see,
Ilk one of them a dozen had
  Well laid on with the tree.

The young men were right swift of foot
  And boldly ran away,
The beggar could them no more hit,
  For all the haste he may.

What ails this haste? the beggar said,
  May ye not tarry still,
Until your money be received ?
  I'll pay you with good will.

The shaking of my pocks, I fear,
  Hath blown into your eyne ;
But I have a good pike-staff here
  Can ripe them out full clean.

The young men answer'd never a word,
  They were dumb as a stane ;
In the thick wood the beggar fled,
  E'er they riped their eyne :

And syne the night became so late,
  To seek him was in vain :
But judge ye, if they lookèd blate,
  When they came home again.

Good Robin spear'd how they had sped,
  They answer'd him, Full ill.
That cannot be, good Robin says,
  Ye have been at the mill.

The mill it is a meatrif place,
  They may lick what they please,
Most like ye have been at that art,
  Who would look to your cloaths.

They hang'd their heads, they dropèd down,
  A word they could not speak.
Robin said, Because I fell a-swoon,
  I think you'll do the like.

Tell on the matter, less or more,
  And tell me where and how,
Ye have done with the bold beggàr
  I sent you for right now.

And when they told him to an end,
  As I have said before,
How that the beggar did them blind,
  What misters process more !

And how he lin'd their shoulders broad
  With his great trenchen tree ; *
And how in the thick wood he fled,
  E'er they a stime could see ;

And how they scarcely could win home,
  Their bones were beft so sore ;

* These two lines are restored from the Aberdeen ballad.

Good Robin cry'd, Fy ! out ! for shame !
  We're sham'd for evermore.

Altho' good Robin would full fain
  Of his wrong revengèd be,
He smil'd to see his merry young men
  Had gotten a taste of the tree.

ROBIN HOOD RESCUING THE WIDOW'S THREE SONS FROM THE SHERIFF,

WHEN GOING TO BE EXECUTED.

This ballad, from a York edition of "Robin Hood's Garland," is one of the oldest extant, and is alluded to in Anthony Munday's play of "The Durnfall of Robert Earl of Huntington." It may not be out of place to premise that the term "silly woman" used in the ballad does not mean foolish, but indicates a combination of virtue and simplicity, in which sense it was sometimes applied to religious persons.

THERE are twelve months in all the year,
  As I hear many say,
But the merriest month in all the year
  Is the merry month of May.

Now Robin Hood is to Nottingham gone,
  With a link a down, and a day,
And there he met a silly old woman,
  Was weeping on the way.

" What news? what news? thou silly old woman,
  What news hast thou for me?"
Said she, there's three squires in Nottingham town,
  To-day are condemned to die.

Robin Hood rescuing the Widow's Three Sons
from the Sheriff.—P. 222.

Oh, have they parishes burnt? he said,
  Or have they ministers slain,
Or have they robbèd any virgin,
  Or with other men's wives have lain?

" They have no parishes burnt, good sir,
  Nor yet have ministers slain,
Nor have they robbèd any virgin,
  Nor with other men's wives have lain."

Oh, what have they done? said Robin Hood,
  I pray thee tell to me.
" It's for slaying of the king's fallow deer,
  Bearing their long bows with thee."

Dost thou not mind, old woman, he said,
  Since thou made me sup and dine?
By the truth of my body, quoth bold Robin Hood
  You could not tell it in better time.

Now Robin Hood is to Nottingham gone,
  With a link, a down, and a day,
And there he met with a silly old palmer,
  Was walking along the highway.

" What news? what news? thou silly old man,
  What news, I do thee pray?"
Said he, three squires in Nottingham town
  Are condemned to die this day.

" Come change thy apparel with me, old man,
  Come change thy apparel for mine;
Here is forty shillings in good silver,
  Go drink it in beer or wine."

Oh, thine apparel is good, he said,
  And mine is ragged and torn;

Wherever you go, wherever you ride,
    Laugh ne'er an old man to scorn.

" Come change thy apparel with me, old churl,
    Come change thy apparel with mine :
Here are twenty pieces of good broad gold,
    Go feast thy brethren with wine."

Then he put on the old man's hat,
    It stood full high on the crown :
" The first bold bargain that I come at,
    It shall make thee come down.'

Then he put on the old man's cloak,
    Was patch'd black, blew, and red ;
He thought it no shame, all the day long,
    To wear the bags of bread.

Then he put on the old man's breeks,
    Was patch'd from ballup to side :
By the truth of my body, bold Robin can say,
    This man lov'd little pride.

Then he put on the old man's hose,
    Were patch'd from knee to wrist : *
By the truth of my body, said bold Robin Hood,
    I'd laugh if I had any list.

Then he put on the old man's shoes,
    Were patch'd both beneath and aboon ;
Then Robin Hood swore a solemn oath,
    It's good habit that makes a man.

* This substitution of the wrist for the ancle is quite
illegitimate, and is used solely for the rhyme. The wrist,
is that joint which wrests or twists, *i.e.* the junction of
the hand and arm, and the term is inapplicable to any
other.

Now Robin Hood is to Nottingham gone,
    With a link a down, and a down,   .
And there he met with the proud sheriff,
    Was walking along the town.

Oh Christ you save, oh, sheriff, he said,
    Oh Christ you save and see ; *
And what will you give to a silly old man
    To-day will your hangman be ?

Some suits, some suits, the sheriff he said,
    Some suits I'll give to thee :
Some suits, some suits, and pence thirteen,
    To-day's a hangman's fee.

Then Robin he turns him round about,
    And jumps from stock to stone :
By the truth of my body, the sheriffe he said
    That's well jumpt, thou nimble old man.

I was ne'er a hangman in all my life,
    Nor yet intend to trade ;
But curst be he, said bold Robin,
    That first a hangman was made.

I've a bag for meal, and a bag for malt,
    And a bag for barley and corn ;
A bag for bread, and a bag for beef,
    And a bag for my little small horn.

I have a horn in my pockèt,
    I got it from Robin Hood,
And still when I set it to my mouth,
    For thee it blows little good.

"Oh, wind thy horn, thou proud fellòw
    Of thee I have no doubt :

      * Regard protect.

Q

I wish that thou give such a blast,
　　Till both thy eyes fall out.''

The first loud blast that he did blow,
　　He blew both loud and shrill.;
A hundred and fifty of Robin Hood's men
　　Came riding over the hill.

The next loud blast that he did give,
　　He blew both loud and amain,
And quickly sixty of Robin Hood's men
　　Came shining over the plain.

Oh, who are those, the sheriff he said,
　　Come tripping over the lee ?
They're my attendants, brave Robin did say,
　　They'll pay a visit to thee.

They took the gallows from the slack,
　　They set it in the glen,
They hang'd the proud sheriff on that,
　　And releas'd their own three men.

Nottingham Castle.—P. 227.

ROBIN HOOD RESCUING THE THREE SQUIRES FROM NOTTINGHAM GALLOWS.

This song, and its tune, as the editor is informed by his ingenious friend, Edward Williams, the Welsh bard, are well known in South Wales, by the name of *Marchog glas*, *i.e.* Green knight. Though apparently ancient, it is not known to exist in black-letter, nor has any better authority been met with than the common Collection of Aldermary-church-yard.—*Ritson.*

BOLD Robin Hood ranging the forrest all round,
   The forrest all round ranged he ;
O there did he meet with a gay lady,
   She came weeping along the highway.

Why weep you, why weep you? bold Robin he said,
   What, weep you for gold or fee ?
Or do you weep for your maidenhead,
   That is taken from your body ?

I weep not for gold, the lady reply'd,
   Neither do I weep for fee ;
Nor do I weep for my maidenhead,
   That is taken from my body.

What weep you for then ? said jolly Robin,
   I prithee come tell unto me.
"Oh ! I do weep for my three sons,
   For they are all condemned to die."

What church have they robb'd? said jolly Robin,
   Or parish-priest have they slain?
What maids have they forc'd against their will?
   Or with other men's wives have lain?

No church have they robb'd, this lady reply'd,
   Nor parish-priest have they slain;
No maids have they forced against their will,
   Nor with other men's wives have lain.

What have they done then? said jolly Robin,
   Come tell me most speedily.
"Oh! it is for killing the king's fallow deer,
   That they are all condemn'd to die."

Get you home, get you home, said jolly Robin,
   Get you home most speedily,
And I will unto fair Nottingham go,
   For the sake of the squires all three.

Then bold Robin Hood for Nottingham goes,
   For Nottingham town goes he,
O there did he meet with a poor beggar-man,
   He came creeping along the highway.

"What news, what news, thou old beggar-man?
   What news, come tell unto me."
"O there's weeping and wailing in Nottingham
     town,
   For the death of the squires all three."

This beggar-man had a coat on his back,
   'Twas neither green, yellow, nor red;
Bold Robin Hood thought 'twas no disgrace
   To be in the beggar-man's stead.

"Come, pull off thy coat, thou old beggar-man,
   And thou shalt put on mine;

And forty good shillings I'll give thee to boot,
  Besides brandy, good beer, ale and wine."

Bold Robin Hood then unto Nottingham came,
  Unto Nottingham town came he ;
O there did he meet with great master sheriff,
  And likewise the squires all three.

One boon, one boon, said jolly Robin,
  One boon I beg on my knee ;
That, as for the death of these three squires,
  Their hangman I may be.

Soon granted, soon granted, says master sheriff,
  Soon granted unto thee ;
And thou shalt have all their gay cloathing,
  Aye, and all their white money.

" Oh, I will have none of their gay cloathing,
  Nor none of their white money,
But I'll have three blasts on my bugle-horn,
  That their souls to heaven may flee."

Then Robin Hood mounted the gallows so high,
  Where he blew loud and shrill,
Till an hundred and ten of Robin Hood's men
  Came marching down the green hill.

Whose men are these ? says master sheriff,
  Whose men are they ? tell unto me.
" O they are mine, but none of thine,
  And are come for the squires all three."

O take them, O take them, says great master
      sheriff,
  O take them along with thee ;
For there's never a man in fair Nottingham,
  Can do the like of thee.

ROBIN HOOD AND ALLIN A DALE.

OR, a pleasant relation how a young gentleman, being in love with a young damsel, she was taken from him to be an old knight's bride: and how Robin Hood, pittying the young man's case, took her from the old knight, when they were going to be marryed, and restored her to her own love again. To a pleasant northern tune, *Robin Hood in the green-wood stood.*

"Bold Robin Hood he did the young man right,
And took the damsel from the doting knight."

From an old black-letter copy in Major Pearson's Collection.—*Ritson.*

COME listen to me, you gallants so free,
  All you that love mirth for to hear,
And I will tell you of a bold outlàw,
  That lived in Nottinghamshire.

As Robin Hood in the forest stood,
  All under the green-wood tree,
There he was aware of a brave young man,
  As fine as fine might be ;

The youngster was cloathed in scarlet red,
  In scarlet fine and gay ;
And he did frisk it over the plain,
  And chanted a round-de-lay.

Robin Hood and Allin a Dale.—P. 230.

As Robin Hood next morning stood
   Amongst the leaves so gay,
There did he espy the same young man,
   Come drooping along the way.

The scarlet he wore the day before
   It was clean cast away ;
And at every step he fetcht a sigh,
   "Alack and a well a day ! "

Then stepped forth brave Little John,
   And Midge the miller's son,
Which made the young man bend his bow,
   When as he see them come.

Stand off, stand off, the young man said,
   What is your will with me ?
" You must come before our master straight,
   Under yon green-wood tree."

And when he came bold Robin Hood before,
   Robin askt him courteously,
O, hast thou any money to spare
   For my merry men and me ?

I have no money, the young man said,
   But five shillings and a ring ;
And that I have kept this seven long years,
   To have it at my wedding.

Yesterday I should have married a maid,
   But she from me was tane,
And chosen to be an old knight's delight,
   Whereby my poor heart is slain.

What is thy name ? then said Robin Hood,
   Come tell me, without any fail.
By the faith of my body, then said the young man,
   My name it is Allin a Dale.

What wilt thou give me, said Robin Hood,
  In ready gold or fee,
To help thee to thy true love again,
  And deliver her unto thee?

I have no money, then quoth the young man,
  No ready gold nor fee,
But I will swear upon a book
  Thy true servant for to be.

"How many miles is it to thy true love?
  Come tell me without guile."
By the faith of my body, then said the young man,
  It is but five little mile.

Then Robin he hasted over the plain,
  He did neither stint nor lin,
Until he came unto the church,
  Where Allin should keep his wedding.

What hast thou here? the bishop then said,
  I prithee now tell unto me.
I am a bold harper, quoth Robin Hood,
  And the best in the north country.

O welcome, O welcome, the bishop he said,
  That musick best pleaseth me.
You shall have no musick, quoth Robin Hood,
  Till the bride and the bridegroom I see.

With that came in a wealthy knight,
  Which was both grave and old,
And after him a finikin lass,
  Did shine like the glistering gold.

This is not a fit match, quoth bold Robin Hood,
  That you do seem to make here,
For since we are come into the church,
  The bride shall chuse her own dear.

Then Robin Hood put his horn to his mouth,
   And blew blasts two or three ;
When four and twenty bowmen bold
   Came leaping over the lee.

And when they came into the church-yard,
   Marching all on a row,
The first man was Allin a Dale,
   To give bold Robin his bow.

This is thy true love, Robin he said,
   Young Allin, as I hear say ;
And you shall be married at this same time,
   Before we depart away.

That shall not be, the bishop he said,
   For thy word shall not stand ;
They shall be three times askt in the church,
   As the law is of our land.

Robin Hood pull'd off the bishop's coat,
   And put it upon Little John ;
By the faith of my body, then Robin said,
   This cloth doth make thee a man.

When Little John went into the quire,
   The people began to laugh ;
He askt them seven times into church,
   Lest three times should not be enough.

Who gives me this maid ? said Little John,
   Quoth Robin Hood, that do I ;
And he that takes her from Allin a Dale,
   Full dearly he shall her buy.

And thus having ended this merry wedding,
   The bride lookt like a queen ;
And so they return'd to the merry green-wood,
   Amongst the leaves so green.

ROBIN HOOD AND THE TINKER.

From an old black-letter copy in the library of Anthony
a Wood. The full title is,

> "A new song to drive away cold winter,
>> Between Robin Hood and the jovial tinker:
>>> How Robin by a wile,
>>> The Tinker he did cheat;
>>> But at the length as you shall hear
>>> The Tinker did him beat,
>>> Whereby the same they did then so agree
>>> They after liv'd in love and unity.
>> To the tune of, *In Summer time.*"

Compared with a ballad in the Roxburgh Collection.

In summer time, when leaves grow green,
Down, a down, a down.
And birds singing on every tree,
Hey down, a down, a down.
Robin Hood went to Nottingham,
As fast as hee could dree.*

And as hee came to Nottingham,
A tinker he did meet,
And seeing him a lusty blade,
He did him kindly greet.

* *Dree* properly signifies to endure or suffer, but is here
explained by Mr. Ritson as *hye*, which means to hasten.

Robin Hood and the Tinker.—P. 234

Where dost thou live? quoth Robin Hood,
   I pray thee now me tell :
Sad news I hear there is abroad,
   I fear all is not well.

What is that news? the tinker said,
   Tell me without delay :
I am a tinker by my trade,
   And do live in Banburay.

As for the news, quoth Robin Hood,
   It is but as I hear,
Two tinkers they were set i'th' stocks,
   For drinking ale and beer.

If that be all, the tinker said,
   As I may say to you,
Your news is not worth a ——,
   Since that they all be true.

For drinking of good ale and beer,
   You will not lose your part.
No, by my faith, quoth Robin Hood,
   I love it with all my heart.

What news abroad? quoth Robin Hood,
   Tell me what thou dost hear :
Seeing thou goest from town to town,
   Some news thou need not fear.

All the news I have, the tinker said,
   I hear it is for good,
It is to seek a bold outlaw,
   Which they call Robin Hood.

I have a warrant from the king,
    To take him where I can ;
If you can tell me where he is,
    I will make you a man.

 he king would give a hundred pound,
    That he could but him see ;
And if we can but now him get,
    It will serve thee and me.

Let me see that warrant, said Robin Hood,
    Ile see if it be right ;
And I will do the best I can
    For to take him this night.

That will I not, the tinker said,
    None with it will I trust ;
And where he is if you'll not tell,
    Take him by force I must.

But Robin Hood perceiving well
    How then the game would go,
" If you would go to Nottingham,
    We shall find him I know."

The tinker had a crab-tree staff,
    Which was both good and strong,
Robin he had a good strong blade ;
    So they went both along.

And when they came to Nottingham,
    There they both tooke an inn ;
And there they call'd for ale and wine,
    To drink it was no sin.

But ale and wine they drank so fast,
    That the tinker he forgot
What thing he was about to do ;
    It fell so to his lot,

That while the tinker fell asleep,
  Robin made then haste away,
And left the tinker in the lurch,
  For the great shot to pay.

But when the tinker wakenèd,
  And saw that he was gone,
He call'd then even for his host,
  And thus he made his moan :

I had a warrant from the king,
  Which might have done me good,
That is to take a bold outlaw,
  Some call him Robin Hood :

But now my warrant and money's gone,
  Nothing I have to pay ;
But he that promis'd to be my friend,
  He's gone and fled away.

That friend you tell on, said the host,
  They call him Robin Hood ;
And when that first he met with you,
  He meant you little good.

"Had I but known it had been he,
  When that I had him here,
Th' one of us should have tri'd our strength,
  Which should have paid full dear.

In the mean time I will away,
  No longer here Ile bide,
But I will go and seek him out,
  Whatever do me betide.

But one thing I would gladly know,
  What here I have to pay ?"
Ten shillings just, then said the host.
  "Ile pay without delay ;

Or else take here my working-bag,
   And my good hammer too ;
And if that I but light on the knave,
   'I will then soon pay you."

The only way, then said the host,
   And not to stand in fear,
Is to seek him among the parks,
   Killing of the king's deer.

The tinker he then went with speed,
   And made then no delay,
Till he had found bold Robin Hood,
   That they might have a fray.

And last he spy'd him in a park,
   Hunting then of the deer ;
What knave is that, quoth Robin Hood,
   That doth come me so near ?

No knave, no knave, the tinker said,
   And that you soon shall know ;
Whether of us hath done most wrong,
   My crab-tree staff shall show.

Then Robin drew his gallant blade,
   Made then of trusty steel ;
But the tinker he laid on so fast,
   That he made Robin reel.

Then Robin's anger did arise,
   He fought right manfully,
Until he had made the tinker
   Almost then fit to fly.

With that they had a bout again,
   They ply'd their weapons fast ;
The tinker thresh'd his bones so sore,
   He made him yeeld at last.

A boon, a boon, Robin he cries,
  If thou will grant it me ;
Before I do it, the tinker said,
  Ile hang thee on this tree.

But the tinker looking him about,
  Robin his horn did blow ;
Then came unto him Little John,
  And William Scadlock too.

What is the matter, quoth Little John,
  You sit on th' highway side ?
"Here is a tinker that stands by,
  That hath paid well my hide."

That tinker then, said Little John,
  Fain that blade I would see,
And I would try what I could do,
  If he'l do as much for me.

But Robin he then wish'd them both
  They should the quarrel cease,
That henceforth we may be as one,
  And ever live in peace.

And for the jovial tinker's part,
  A hundred pounds Ile give
In th' year for to maintain him on,
  As long as he doth live.

In manhood he is a mettle-man,
  And a metal-man by trade ;
Never thought I that any man
  Should have made me so afraid.

And if he will be one of us,
  We will take all one fare ;
And whatsoever we do get,
  He shall have his full share.

So the tinker was content
　With them to go along,
And with them a part to take :
　And so I end my song.
　　　Hey down, &c.

Robin Hood and the Bishop.—P. 140.

ROBIN HOOD AND THE RANGER;

OR, TRUE FRIENDSHIP AFTER A FIERCE FIGHT.

No ancient copy of this ballad having been met with, it is
given from an edition of " Robin Hood's Garland," printed
some years since at York.   The tune is *Arthur a Bland.—
Ritson.*

WHEN Phœbus had melted the 'sickles of ice,
    With a hey down, &c.
And likewise the mountains of snow,
Bold Robin Hood he would ramble away,
    To frolick abroad with his bow.

He left all his merry men waiting behind,
    Whilst through the green vallies he pass'd,
Where he did behold a forester bold,
    Who cry'd out, Friend, whither so fast ?

I am going, quoth Robin, to kill a fat buck,
    For me and my merry men all ;
Besides, ere I go, I'll have a fat doe,
    Or else it shall cost me a fall.

You'd best have a care, said the forester then,
    For these are his majesty's deer ;
Before you shall shoot, the thing I'll dispute,
    For I am head forester here.

These thirteen long summers, quoth Robin, I'm
        sure,
    My arrows I here have let fly,

R

Where freely I range ; methinks it is strange,
   You should have more power than I.

This forest, quoth Robin, I think is my own,
   And so are the nimble deer too ;
Therefore I declare, and solemnly swear,
   I'll not be affronted by you.

The forester he had a long quarter staff,
   Likewise a broad sword by his side ;
Without more ado, he presently drew,
   Declaring the truth should be try'd.

Bold Robin Hood had a sword of the best,
   Thus, ere he would take any wrong,
His courage was flush, he'd venture a brush,
   And thus they fell to it ding dong.

The very first blow that the forester gave,
   He made his broad weapon cry twang ;
'Twas over the head, he fell down for dead,
   O that was a damnable bang !

But Robin he soon recover'd himself,
   And bravely fell to it again ;
The very next stroke their weapons they broke
   Yet never a man there was slain.

At quarter staff then they resolvèd to play,
   Because they would have t'other bout ;
And brave Robin Hood right valiantly stood,
   Unwilling he was to give out.

Bold Robin he gave him very hard blows,
   The other return'd them as fast ;
At every stroke their jackets did smoke ;
   Three hours the combat did last.

At length in a rage the forester grew,
   And cudgell'd bold Robin so sore,
That he could not stand, so shaking his hand,
   He cry'd, let us freely give o'er.

Thou art a brave fellow, I needs must confess,
   I never knew any so good ;
Thou art fitting to be a yeoman for me,
   And range in the merry green-wood.

I'll give thee this ring as a token of love,
   For bravely thou hast acted thy part ;
That man that can fight, in him I delight,
   And love him with all my whole heart.

Robin Hood set his bugle horn to his mouth,
   A blast then he merrily blows ;
His yeomen did hear, and strait did appear,
   A hundred with trusty long bows.

Now Little John came at the head of them all,
   Cloth'd in a rich mantle of green ;
And likewise the rest were gloriously drest,
   A delicate sight to be seen !

Lo ! these are my yeomen, said bold Robin Hood,
   And thou shalt be one of the train ;
A mantle and bow, and quiver also,
   I give them whom I entertain.

The forester willingly enter'd the list,
   They were such a beautiful sight ;
Then with a long bow they shot a fat doe,
   And made a rich supper that night.

What singing and dancing was in the green wood,
   For joy of another new mate !
With might and delight they spent all the night
   And liv'd at a plentiful rate.

The forester ne'er was so merry before,
   As then he was with these brave souls,
Who never would fail, in wine, beer, or ale,
   To take off their cherishing bowls.

Then Robin Hood gave him a mantle of green,
   Broad arrows and curious long bow :
This done, the next day, so gallant and gay,
   He marchèd them all in a row.

Quoth he, my brave yeomen, be true to your
     trust,
   And then we may range the woods wide.
They all did declare, and solemnly swear,
   They would conquer, or die by his side.

Robin Hood and the Bishop of Hereford.—P. 245.

ROBIN HOOD AND THE BISHOP OF HEREFORD.

THIS excellent ballad, given from the common edition o Aldermary church-yard (compared with the York copy), is supposed to be modern : the story, however, seems alluded to in the ballad of "Renowned Robin Hood." The full title is "The bishop of Hereford's entertainment by Robin Hood and Little John, &c. in merry Barnsdale."—*Ritson.*

SOME they will talk of bold Robin Hood,
  And some of barons bold ;
But I'll tell you how he serv'd the Bishop of
    Hereford,
When he robb'd him of his gold.

As it befel in merry Barnsdale,
  All under the green-wood tree,
The Bishop of Hereford was to come by,
  With all his company.

Come, kill me a ven'son, said bold Robin Hood,
  Come, kill me a good fat deer,
The bishop of Hereford is to dine with me to-day,
  And he shall pay well for his cheer.

We'll kill a fat ven'son, said bold Robin Hood,
  And dress it by the highway side ;
And we will watch the bishop narrowly,
  Lest some other way he should ride.

Robin Hood dress'd himself in shepherd's attire,
  With six of his men also;
And, when the bishop of Hereford came by,
  They about the fire did go.

O what is the matter? then said the bishòp,
  Or for whom do you make this a-do?
Or why do you kill the king's ven'son,
  When your company is so few?

We are shephèrds, said bold Robin Hood,
  And we keep sheep all the year,
And we are disposed to be merry this day,
  And to kill of the king's fat deer.

You are brave fellows! said the bishop,
  And the king of your doings shall know:
Therefore make haste, and come along with me,
  For before the king you shall go.

O pardon, O pardon, said bold Robin Hood,
  O pardon, I thee pray!
For it becomes not your lordship's coat
  To take so many lives away.

No pardon, no pardon, said the bishòp,
  No pardon I thee owe;
Therefore make haste, and come along with me,
  For before the king you shall go.

Then Robin set his back 'gainst a tree,
  And his foot against a thorn,
And from underneath his shepherd's coat
  He pull'd out a bugle horn.

He put the little end to his mouth,
  And a loud blast did he blow,
Till threescore and ten of bold Robin's men
  Came running all on a row:

All making obeysance to bold Robin Hood,
  'Twas a comely sight for to see.
What is the matter, master, said Little John,
  That you blow so hastilie?

" O here is the bishop of Hereford,
  And no pardon we shall have."
Cut off his head, master, said Little John,
  And throw him into his grave.

O pardon, O pardon, said the bishòp,
  O pardon, I thee pray ;
For if I had known it had been you,
  I'd have gone some other way.

No pardon, no pardon, said bold Robin Hood,
  No pardon I thee owe ;
Therefore make haste, and come along with me,
  For to merry Barnsdale you shall go.

Then Robin he took the bishop by the hand,
  And led him to merry Barnsdale ;
He made him to stay and sup with him that
    night,
  And to drink wine, beer, and ale.

Call in a reckoning, said the bishòp,
  For méthinks it grows wond'rous high.
Lend me your purse, master, said Little John,
  And I'll tell you bye and bye.

Then Little John took the bishop's cloak,
  And spread it upon the ground,
And out of the bishop's portmantua
  He told three hundred pound.

Here's money enough, master, said Little John,
　And a comely sight 'tis to see ;
It makes me in charity with the bishop,
　Tho' he heartily loveth not me.

Robin Hood took the bishop by the hand,
　And he caused the music to play ;
And he made the [old] bishop to dance in his
　　boots,
　And glad he could so get away.

The King's disguise; and Friendship with Robin Hood.—P. 249.

THE KING'S DISGUISE, AND FRIEND-SHIP WITH ROBIN HOOD.

TAKEN by Mr. Ritson from the common Collection of Aldermary church-yard, and now compared with one in the York edition.

KING Richard hearing of the pranks
  Of Robin Hood and his men,
He much admir'd, and more desir'd,
  To see both him and them.

Then with a dozen of his lords,
  To Nottingham he rode ;
When he came there, he made good cheer,
  And took up his abode.

He having stayèd there some time,
  But had no hopes to speed,
He and his lords, with one accord,
  All put on monks' weeds.

From Fountain's-abbey they did ride,
  Down to Barnesdale ;
Where Robin Hood preparèd stood,
  All company to assail.

The king was higher than the rest,
  And Robin thought, he had
An abbot been whom he had seen,
  To rob him he was glad.

He took the king's horse by the head,
  Abbot, says he, abide ;
I am bound to sue such knaves as you,
  That live in pomp and pride.

But we are messengers from the king,
  The king himself did say ;
Near to this place his royal grace
  To speak with thee does stay.

God save the king, said Robin Hood,
  And all that wish him well ;
He that denies his sovereignty,
  I wish he was in hell.

Thyself thou cursedst, said the king,
  For thou a traitor art.
" Nay, but that you are his messenger,
  I swear you lie in heart ;

For I never yet hurt any man
  That honest is and true ;
But those who give their minds to live
  Upon other men's due.

I never hurt the husbandmen,
  That use to till the ground :
Nor spill their blood who range the wood,
  To follow hawk or hound.

My chiefest spite to clergy is,
  Who in these days bear sway ;
With fryars and monks, and their fine spunks,
  I make my chiefest prey.

But I am glad, says Robin Hood,
  That I have met you here ;
Before we end, you shall, my friend,
  Taste of our green-wood cheer."

The king he then did marvel much,
 And so did all his men ;
They thought with fear, what kind of cheer,
 Robin would provide for them.

Robin took the king's horse by the head,
 And led him to his tent :
Thou shouldst not be so us'd, quoth he,
 But that my king thee sent.

Nay, more than that, quoth Robin Hood,
 For good king Richard's sake,
If you had as much gold as ever I told,
 I would not one penny take.

Then Robin set his horn to his mouth,
 And a loud blast he did blow,
Till a hundred and ten of Robin Hood's men,
 Came marching all of a row.

And when they came bold Robin before,
 Each man did bend his knee :
O, thought the king, 'tis a gallant thing,
 And a seemly sight to see.

Within himself the king did say,
 These men of Robin Hood's
More humble be than mine to me ;
 So the court may learn of the woods.

So then they all to dinner went,
 Upon a carpet green ;
Black, yellow, red, finely minglèd,
 Most curious to be seen.

Venison and fowls were plenty there,
 With fish out of the river :
King Richard swore, on sea or shore,
 He never was feasted better.

Then Robin takes a can of ale :
   " Come, let us now begin ;
And every man shall have his can :
   Here's a health unto the king."

The king himself drank to the king,
   So round about it went ;
Two barrels of ale, both stout and stale,
   To pledge that health was spent.

And, after that, a bowl of wine
   In his hand took Robin Hood ;
Until I die, I'll drink wine, said he,
   While I live in the green-wood.

Bend all your bows, said Robin Hood,
   And with the grey goose-wing,
Such sport now show, as you would do
   In the presence of the king.

They shewed such brave archery,
   By cleaving sticks and wands,
That the king did say, such men as they
   Live not in many lands.

Well, Robin Hood, then says the king,
   If I could thy pardon get,
To serve the king in every thing
   Wouldst thou thy mind firm set ?

Yes, with all my heart, bold Robin said,
   So they flung off their hoods,
To serve the king in every thing,
   They swore they would spend their bloods.

For a clergyman was first my bane,
   Which makes me hate them all,
But if you will be so kind to me,
   Love them again I shall.

The king no longer could forbear,
  For he was mov'd with ruth,
Robin, said he, I'll now tell thee
  The very naked truth.

" I am the king, thy sovereign king,
  That appears before you all."
When Robin saw that it was he,
  Strait then he down did fall.

Stand up again, then said the king,
  I'll thee thy pardon give ;
Stand up, my friend ; who can contend,
  When I give leave to live ?

So they are all gone to Nottingham,
  All shouting as they came :
But when the people them did see,
  They thought the king was slain ;

And for that cause th' outlaws were come.
  To rule all as they list ;
And them to shun, which way to run
  The people did not wist.

The plowman left the plow in the field,
  The smith ran from his shop ;
Old folks also, that scarce could go,
  Over their sticks did hop.

The king did soon let them understand
  He had been in the green-wood,
And from that day, for evermore,
  He'd forgiven Robin Hood.

Then when the people they did hear,
  And that the truth was known,
They all did sing, God save the king !
  Hang care, the town's our own !

What's that Robin Hood ? then said the sheriff,
    That varlet I do hate !
Both me and mine he caus'd to dine,
    And serv'd us all with one plate.

Ho, ho, said Robin Hood, I know what you mean,
    Come, take your gold again ;
Be friends with me, and I with thee,
    And so with every man.

Now, master sheriff, you are paid,
    And since you are beginner,
And well as you give me my due,
    For you ne'er paid for that dinner.

But if that it should please the king,
    So much your house to grace,
To sup with you, for, to speak true,
    I know you ne'er was base.

The sheriff could not that gainsay,
    For a trick was put upon him ;
A supper was drest, the king was a guest,
    But he thought 'twould have outdone him.

They are all gone to London court,
    Robin Hood, with all his train ;
He once was there a noble peer,
    And now he's there again.

Many such pranks brave Robin play'd,
    While he liv'd in the green-wood :
Now, my friend, attend, and hear an end
    Of honest Robin Hood.

Robin Hood and the Golden Arrow.—P. 255.

ROBIN HOOD AND THE GOLDEN ARROW

FROM the Aldermary church-yard Collection.

WHEN as the sheriff of Nottingham
    Was come with mickle grief,
He talk'd no good of Robin Hood,
    That strong and sturdy thief.
        Fal la dal de.

So unto London road he past,
    His losses to unfold
To king Richàrd, who did regard
    The tale that he had told.

Why, quoth the king, what shall I do!
    Art thou not sheriff for me?
The law is in force, to take its course
    Of them that injure thee.

Go get thee gone, and by thyself
    Devise some tricking game,
For to enthral yon rebels all;
    Go take thy course with them.

So away the sheriff he return'd,
    And by the way he thought
Of th' words of the king, and how the thing
    To pass might well be brought.

For within his mind he imaginèd,
   That when such matches were,
Those outlaws stout, without all doubt,
   Would be the bowmen there.

So an arrow with a golden head,
   And shaft of silver-white,
Who on the day should bear away
   For his own proper right.

Tidings came to bold Robin Hood,
   Under the green-wood tree :
"Come prepare you then, my merry men,
   We'll go yon sport to see."

With that stept forth a brave young man,
   David of Doncaster,
Master, said he, be rul'd by me,
   From the green-wood we'll not stir.

To tell the truth, I'm well inform'd,
   Yon match it is a wile ;
The sheriff, I wiss, devises this
   Us archers to beguile.

Thou smells of a coward, said Robin Hood,
   Thy words do not please me ;
Come on't what will, I'll try my skill,
   At yon brave archery.

O then bespoke brave Little John,
   Come let us thither gang ;
Come, listen to me, how it shall be,
   That we need not be kenn'd.

Our mantles all of Lincoln-green
   Behind us we will leave ;
We'll dress us all so several,
   They shall us not perceive.

One shall wear white, another red,
  One yellow, another blue ;
Thus in disguise, to the exercise
  We'll gang, whate'er ensue.

Forth from the green-wood they are gone,
  With hearts all firm and stout,
Resolving then with the sheriff's men
  To have a hearty bout.

So themselves they mixèd with the rest,
  To prevent all suspicion ;
For if they should together hold
  They thought it no discretion.

So the sheriff looked round about,
  Amongst eight hundred men,
But could not see the sight that he
  Had long suspected then.

Some said, if Robin Hood was here,
  And all his men to boot,
Sure none of them could pass these men,
  So bravely do they shoot.

Ay, quoth the sheriff, and scratch'd his head,
  I thought he would have been here ;
I thought he would, but tho' he's bold,
  He durst not now appear.

O that word griev'd Robin Hood to the heart,
  He vexèd in his blood ;
Ere long, thought he, thou shalt well see
  That here was Robin Hood.

Some cried, Blue jacket! another cried, Brown
  And a third cried, brave Yellow !
But the fourth man said, Yon man in Red
  In this place has no fellow.

s

For that was Robin Hood himself,
　　For he was cloath'd in red ;
At every shot the prize he got,
　　For he was both sure and dead.

So the arrow with the golden head,
　　And shaft of silver-white,
Brave Robin Hood won, and bore with him,
　　For his own proper right.

These outlaws there, that very day
　　To shun all kinds of doubt,
By three or four, no less nor more,
　　As they went in came out ;

Until they all assembled were
　　Under the green-wood shade,
Where they report, in pleasant sport,
　　What brave pastime they made.

Says Robin Hood, all my care is,
　　How that yon sheriff may
Know certainly that it was I,
　　That bore his arrow away.

Says Little John, my counsel good
　　Did take effect before,
So therefore now, if you'll allow,
　　I will advise once more.

Speak on, speak on, said Robin Hood,
　　Thy wit's both quick and sound,
I know no man among us can
　　For wit like thee be found.

This I advise, said Little John,
　　That a letter shall be penn'd,
And when it is done, to Nottingham
　　You to the sheriff shall send.

That is well advis'd, said Robin Hood,
   But how must it be sent?
"Pugh! when you please, 'tis done with ease;
   Master, be you content.

I'll stick it on my arrow's head,
   And shoot it into the town ;
The mark will show where it must go,
   Whenever it lights down."

The project it was well perform'd,
   The sheriff that letter had,
Which when he read, he scratch'd his head,
   And rav'd like one that's mad.

So we'll leave him chafing in his grease,
   Which will do him no good :
Now, my friends, attend, and hear the end
   Of honest Robin Hood.

ROBIN HOOD AND LITTLE JOHN.

BEING an account of their first meeting, their fierce encounter, and conquest. To which is added, their friendly
agreement; and how he came to be called Little John.
Tune of *Arthur a Bland*.

This ballad is named in a schedule of such things under
an agreement between W. Thackeray and others in 1689,
(Coll. Pepys, vol. v.), but is here given as corrected from
a copy in the "Collection of Old Ballads," 1723. See
preface, pp. xiii. xiv. &c. for an account of Little John,
also in the "Collection of Old Ballads," vol. i. p. 75.

WHEN Robin Hood was about twenty years old;
  With a hey down, down, and a down;
He happen'd to meet with Little John,
A jolly brisk blade, right fit for the trade,
 For he was a lusty young man.

Tho' he was call'd Little, his limbs they were large,
 And his stature was seven foot high;
Wherever he came, they quak'd at his name,
 For soon he would make them to fly.

How they came acquainted, I'll tell you in brief,
 If you would but listen awhile;
For this very jest, among all the rest,
 I think it may cause you to smile.

For Robin Hood said to his jolly bowmèn.
 Pray tarry you here in this grove;

Robin Hood and Little John.—P. 260.

And see that you all observe well my call,
  While through the forest I rove.

We have had no sport for these fourteen long days,
  Therefore now abroad will I go ;
Now should I be beat, and cannot retreat,
  My horn I will presently blow.

Then did he shake hands with his merry men all,
  And bid them at present good bye :
Then, as near the brook his journey he took,
  A stranger he chanc'd to espy.

They happen'd to meet on a long narrow bridge,
  And neither of them would give way ;
Quoth bold Robin Hood, and sturdily stood,
  I'll shew you right Nottingham play.

With that from his quiver an arrow he drew,
  A broad arrow with a goose-wing.
The stranger replied, I'll liquor thy hide,
  If thou offer to touch the string.

Quoth bold Robin Hood, thou dost prate like an
    ass,
  For were I to bend but my bow,
I could send a dart quite thro' thy proud heart,
  Before thou couldst strike me one blow.

Thou talk'st like a coward, the stranger reply'd ;
  Well arm'd with a long bow you stand,
To shoot at my breast, while I, I protest,
  Have nought but a staff in my hand.

The name of a coward, quoth Robin, I scorn,
  Therefore my long bow I'll lay by ;
And now, for thy sake, a staff will I take,
  The truth of thy manhood to try.

Then Robin Hood stept to a thicket of trees,
   And chose him a staff of brown oak;
Now this being done, away he did run
   To the stranger, and merrily spoke:

Lo! see my staff is lusty and tough,
   Now here on this bridge we will play;
Whoever falls in, the other shall win
   The battle, and so we'll away.

With all my whole heart, the stranger reply'd,
   I scorn in the least to give out;
This said, they fell to't without more dispute,
   And their staffs they did flourish about.

At first Robin he gave the stranger a bang,
   So hard that he made his bones ring:
The stranger he said, this must be repaid,
   I'll give you as good as you bring.

So long as I am able to handle a staff,
   To die in your debt, friend, I scorn.
Then to it each goes, and follow'd their blows,
   As if they'd been threshing of corn.

The stranger gave Robin a crack on the crown,
   Which caused the blood to appear;
Then Robin enrag'd, more fiercely engag'd,
   And follow'd his blows more severe.

So thick and so fast did he lay it on him,
   With a passionate fury and ire;
At every stroke he made him to smoke,
   As if he had been all on fire.

O then into fury the stranger he grew,
   And gave him a damnable look,
And with it a blow that laid him full low,
   And tumbled him into the brook.

I prithee, good fellow, O where art thou now?
   The stranger, in laughter, he cry'd.
Quoth bold Robin Hood, good faith, in the flood,
   And floating along with the tide.

I needs must acknowledge thou art a brave soul,
   With thee I'll no longer contend ;
For needs must I say, thou hast got the day,
   Our battle shall be at an end.

Then unto the bank he did presently wade,
   And pull'd himself out by a thorn ;
Which done, at the last, he blew a loud blast
   Straitway on his fine bugle-horn :

The echo of which through the valleys did fly,
   At which his stout bowmen appear'd,
All clothed in green, most gay to be seen,
   So up to their master they steer'd.

O, what's the matter? quoth William Stutely ;
   Good master, you are wet to the skin.
No matter, quoth he, the lad which you see
   In fighting hath tumbled me in.

He shall not go scot-free, the others reply'd ;
   So strait they were seizing him there,
To duck him likewise : but Robin Hood cries,
   He is a stout fellow ; forbear.

There's no one shall wrong thee, friend, be not
     afraid ;
   These bowmen upon me do wait ;
There's threescore and nine ; if thou wilt be mine,
   Thou shalt have my livery strait,

And other accoutrements fitting also :
   Speak up, jolly blade, never fear.

I'll teach you also the use of the bow,
    To shoot at the fat fallow deer.

O, here is my hand, the stranger reply'd,
    I'll serve you with all my whole heart ;
My name is John Little, a man of good mettle :
    Ne'er doubt it, for I'll play my part.

His name shall be alter'd, quoth William Stutely,
    And I will his godfather be ;
Prepare then a feast, and none of the least,
    For we will be merry, quoth he.

They presently fetch'd him a brace of fat does,
    With humming strong liquor likewise ;
They lov'd what was good ; so, in the green-wood,
    This pretty sweet babe they baptize.

He was, I must tell you, but seven foot high,
    And, may be, an ell in the waist ;
A sweet pretty lad : much feasting they had :
    Bold Robin the christ'ning grac'd,

With all his bowmèn, who stood in a ring,
    And were of the Nottingham breed ;
Brave Stutely came then, with seven yeomèn,
    And did in this manner proceed :

This infant was called John Little, quoth he ;
    His name shall be changed anon :
The words we'll transpose ; so wherever he goes,
    His name shall be call'd Little John.

They all with a shout made the elements ring ;
    So soon as the office was o'er,
To feasting they went, with true merriment,
    And tippled strong liquor galore.

Then Robin he took the pretty sweet babe,
  And cloth'd him from top to toe,
In garments of green, most gay to be seen,
  And gave him a curious long bow.

"Thou shalt be an archer as well as the best,
  And range in the green-wood with us ;
Where we'll not want gold nor silver, behold,
  While bishops have aught in their purse.

"We live here like 'squires, or lords of renown,
  Without e'er a foot of free land ;
We feast on good cheer, with wine, ale, and beer,
  And ev'ry thing at our command."

Then music and dancing did finish the day ;
  At length, when the sun waxed low,
Then all the whole train the grove did refrain,
  And unto their caves they did go.

And so ever after, as long as he liv'd,
  Altho' he was proper and tall,
Yet, nevertheless, the truth to express,
  Still Little John they do him call.

ROBIN HOOD AND MAID MARIAN.

THIS ballad is given from an old black-letter copy in the Collection of Anthony à Wood. Its full title is "A famous battle between Robin Hood and maid Marian; declaring their love, life, and liberty. Tune, *Robin Hood reviv'd.*" —*Ritson.*

This ballad is evidently founded upon incidents in the play of "The Downfall of Robert Earl of Huntington."

A BONNY fine-maid of a noble degree,
    With a hey down, down, a down, down,
Maid Marian call'd by name,
Did live in the North, of excellent worth,
    For she was a gallant dame.

For favour and face, and beauty most rare,
    Queen Helen she did excell:
For Marian then was prais'd of all men
    That did in the country dwell.

'Twas neither Rosamond nor Jane Shore,
    Whose beauty was clear and bright,
That could surpass this country lass,
    Beloved of lord and knight.

The earl of Huntington, nobly born,
    That came of noble blood,
To Marian went, with a good intent,
    By the name of Robin Hood.

Robin Hood and Maid Marian.—P. 266.

With kisses sweet their red lips meet,
  For she and the earl did agree ;
In every place, they kindly embrace,
  With love and sweet unity.

But fortune bearing these lovers a spite,
  That soon they were forc'd to part :
To the merry green-wood then went Robin Hood,
  With a sad and sorrowfull heart.

And Marian, poor soul, was troubled in mind,
  For the absence of her friend ;
With finger in eye, she often did cry,
  And his person did much commend.

Perplexed and vexed, and troubled in mind,
  She drest herself like a page,
And ranged the wood, to find Robin Hood,
  The bravest of men in that age.

With quiver and bow, sword, buckler, and all,
  Thus armed was Marian most bold,
Still wandering about, to find Robin out,
  Whose person was better than gold.

But Robin Hood, he, himself had disguis'd,
  And Marian was strangely attir'd,
That they prov'd foes, and so fell to blows,
  Whose valour bold Robin admir'd.

They drew out their swords, to cutting they went,
  At least an hour or more,
That the blood ran apace from bold Robin's face,
  And Marian was wounded sore.

O hold thy hand, hold thy hand, said Robin Hood,
  And thou shalt be one of my string,
To range in the wood, with bold Robin Hood,
  To hear the sweet nightingall sing.

When Marian did hear the voice of her love,
    Her self she did quickly discover,
And with kisses so sweet she did soon him greet,
    Like to a most loyall lover.

When bold Robin Hood his Marian did see,
    Good lord, what clipping was there !
With kind embraces, and jobbing of faces,
    Providing of gallant cheer.

For Little John took his bow in his hand,
    And wand'ring in the wood,
To kill the deer, and make good chear,
    For Marian and Robin Hood.

THE SECOND PART.

A stately banquet they had full soon,
    All in a shaded bower,
Where venison sweet they had to eat,
    And were merry that present hour.

Great flaggons of wine were set on the board,
    And merrily they drunk round
Their boules of sack, to strengthen the back,
    Whilst their knees did touch the ground.

First Robin Hood began a health
    To Marian his onely dear ;
And his yeomen all, both comly and tall,
    Did quickly bring up the rear :

For in a brave vent they tost off the bouls,
   Whilst thus they did remain ;
And every cup, as they drunk up,
   They filled with speed again.

At last they ended their merryment,
   And went to walk in the wood,
Where Little John, and maid Mariàn,
   Attended on bold Robin Hood.

In solid content together they liv'd,
   With all their yeomen gay ;
They liv'd by their hands, without any lands,
   And so they did many a day.

But now to conclude, an end I will make,
   In time as I think it good ;
For the people that dwell in the north can tell
   Of Marian and bold Robin Hood.

ROBIN HOOD AND THE VALIANT KNIGHT.

TOGETHER with an account of his death and burial, &c. Tune of *Robin Hood and the fifteen foresters.* From the common garland of Aldermary church-yard; corrected by the York copy.

WHEN Robin Hood, and his merry men all,
     Derry down, down,
  Had reigned many years,
The king was then told, that they had been bold
  To his bishops and noble peers.
     Hey down, derry, derry down.

Therefore they called a council of state,
  To know what was best to be done,
For to quell their pride, or else they reply'd
  The land would be over-run.

Having consulted a whole summer's day,
  At length it was agreed,
That one should be sent to try the event,
  And fetch him away with speed.

Therefore a trusty and most worthy knight
  The king was pleased to call,
Sir William by name; when to him he came,
  He told him his pleasure all.

" Go you from hence to bold Robin Hood,
    And bid him without more ado,
Surrender himself, or else the proud elf
    Shall suffer with all his crew.

Take here a hundred bowmen brave,
    All chosen men of great might,
Of excellent art to take thy part,
    In glittering armour most bright."

Then said the knight, my sovereign liege,
    By me they shall be led ;
I'll venture my blood against bold Robin Hood,
    And bring him alive or dead.

One hundred men were chosen straight,
    As proper as e'er men saw :
On Midsummer-day they march'd away,
    To conquer that brave outlaw.

With long yew bows, and shining spears,
    They march'd with mickle pride,
And never delay'd, nor halted, nor stay'd
    Till they came to the green-wood side.

Said he to his archers, tarry here,
    Your bows make ready all,
That if need should be, you may follow me,
    And see you observe my call.

I'll go first in person, he cry'd,
    With the letters of my good king,
Wel' sign'd and seal'd, and if he will yield,
    We need not draw one string.

He wander'd about till at length he came
    To the tent of Robin Hood;
The letter he shows ; bold Robin arose,
    And there on his guard he stood.

They'd have me surrender, quoth bold Robin Hood,
   And lie at their mercy then;
But tell them from me, that never shall be,
   While I have full seven score men.

Sir William the knight, both hardy and bold,
   He offer'd to seize him there,
Which William Locksley by fortune did see,
   And bid him that trick to forbear.

Then Robin Hood set his horn to his mouth,
   And blew a blast or twain,
And so did the knight, at which there in sight
   The archers came all amain.

Sir William with care he drew up his men,
   And plac'd them in battle array;
Bold Robin, we find, he was not behind:
   Now this was a bloody fray.

The archers on both sides bent their bows,
   And the clouds of arrows flew;
The very first flight, that honour'd knight
   Did there bid the world adieu.

Yet nevertheless their fight did last
   From morning till almost noon;
Both parties were stout and loth to give out,
   This was on the last day of June.

At length they left off: one party they went
   To London with right good will;
And Robin Hood he to the green-wood tree,
   And there he was taken ill.

He sent for a monk, to let him blood,
   Who took his life away:
Now this being done, his archers they run,
   It was not a time to stay.

Some got on board, and cross'd the seas,
  To Flanders, France, and Spain,
And others to Rome, for fear of their doom,
  But soon return'd again.

This account of Robin Hood's death differs from all
other reports, particularly from that contained in the next
ensuing ballad, which is not only more ancient, but accords
with others that appear much more authentic, if authen-
ticity is now attainable.

Mr. Douce, in his copy in the Bodleian Library, has
added the following note :—

" In the Bishop of Dromore's celebrated manuscript of
Ancient Poetry, from which a great part of his collections
was printed, is a fragment of a ballad, which makes Robin
Hood to have been treacherously let blood by his aunt
the prioress of Kirklees."

The following Lament is taken from Collier's edition of
the play of *The Death of Robert Earl of Huntington :—*

" Weep, weep, ye woodmen wail,
  Your hands with sorrow wring ;
  Your master, Robin Hood, lies dead,
  Therefore sigh as you sing.
Here lie his primer and his beads,
His bent bow and his arrows keen ;
His good sword and his holy cross,
Now cast on flowers fresh and green.
  And as they fall shed tears and say,
  Well, well-a-day, well-a, well-a-day ;
  Thus cast ye flowers and sing,
  And on to Wakefield take your way."

ROBIN HOOD'S DEATH AND BURIAL.

This very old and curious piece is preserved solely in the editions of "Robin Hood's Garland," printed at York, where it is made to conclude with some foolish lines (adopted from the London copy of the preceding ballad), in order to introduce the epitaph. It is here given from a collation of two different copies, containing numerous variations.

WHEN Robin Hood and Little John,
  Down a down, a down, a down,
Went o'er yon bank of broom,
Said Robin Hood to Little John,
 We have shot for many a pound :
  Hey down, a down, a down.

But I am not able to shoot one shot more,
 My arrows will not flee ;
·But I have a cousin lives down below,
 Please God, she will bleed me.

Now Robin is to fair Kirkley gone,
 As fast as he can wen ;
But before he came there, as we do hear,
 He was taken very ill.

And when that he came to fair Kirkley-hall,
 He knock'd all at the ring,

But none was so ready as his cousin herself
   For to let bold Robin in.

Will you please to sit down, cousin Robin, she said,
   And drink some beer with me ?
"No, I will neither eat nor drink,
   Till I am blooded by thee."

Well, I have a room, cousin Robin, she said,
   Which you did never see,
And if you please to walk therein,
   You blooded by me shall be.

She took him by the lily-white hand,
   And led him to a private room,
And there she blooded bold Robin Hood,
   Whilst one drop of blood would run.

She blooded him in the vein of the arm,
   And lock'd him up in the room,
There did he bleed all the live-long day,
   Until the next day at noon.

He then bethought him of a casement door,
   Thinking for to be gone,
He was so weak he could not leap,
   Nor could he get him down.

He then bethought him of his bugle-horn,
   Which hung low down to his knee,
He set his horn unto his mouth,
   And blew out weak blasts three.

Then Little John, when hearing him,
   As he sat under the tree,
"I fear my master is near dead,
   He blows so wearily."

Then Little John to fair Kirkley is gone,
  As fast as he can dree;
But when he came to Kirkley-hall,
  He broke locks two or three:

Until he came bold Robin to,
  Then he fell on his knee;
A boon, a boon, cries Little John,
  Master. I beg of thee.

What is that boon, quoth Robin Hood,
  Little John, thou begs of me?
"It is to burn fair Kirkley-hall,
  And all their nunnery."

Now nay, now nay, quoth Robin Hood,
  That boon I'll not grant thee;
I never hurt woman in all my life,
  Nor man in woman's company.

I never hurt fair maid in all my time,
  Nor at my end shall it be;
But give me my bent bow in my hand,
  And a broad arrow I'll let flee;
And where this arrow is taken up,
  There shall my grave ligg'd be.

Lay me a green sod under my head,
  And another at my feet;
And lay my bent bow by my side,
  Which was my music sweet;
And make my grave of gravel and green,
  Which is most right and meet.

Let me have length and breadth enough,
  With a green sod under my head;
That they may say, when I am dead,
  Here lies bold Robin Hood.

These words they readily promis'd him,
  Which did bold Robin please:
And there they buried bold Robin Hood,
  Near to the fair Kirklèys.

ADAM BELL, CLYM OF THE CLOUGH, AND WILLYAM OF CLOUDESLE.

THIS popular legend is undoubtedly entitled to a place in the cycle of "Robin Hood ballads," whether these yeomen were contemporaries, or not, with Robin Hood and his companions. They were three noted outlaws, whose skill in archery rendered them as famous in the north of England, as Robin Hood and his fellows were in the midland counties.

"This very ancient, curious, and popular performance, apparently composed for the purpose of being sung in public to the harp, is extant in an old quarto, in black-letter, without date, 'Imprinted at London, in Lothburye, by Wyllyam Copland,' and preserved among Mr. Garrick's Old Plays, now in the British Museum, whence it is here given.

"The 'Englishe wood' mentioned in v. 16, &c. is Englewood or Inglewood, an extensive forest in Cumberland, which was sixteen miles in length, and reached from Carlisle to Penrith. A similar observation has been already made by Dr. Percy, who adds, that 'Engle or Ingle-wood signifies wood for firing.' But, with submission to so good a judge, it should rather seem, in the present instance, to design a wood or forest in which extraordinary fires were made on particular occasions; a conjecture which will appear the more plausible, when it is considered that the identical spot on which Penrith beacon now stands, and where a beacon has stood for ages, was formerly within the limits of this very forest; and that Ingleborough, one of 'the highest hills between Scotland and Trent,' has ob tained this name from the fires anciently lighted in the beacon erected on its flat top, where the foundation is still visible."

> MERY it was in grene forest,
> Amonge the leues grene,

Wher that men walk east and west,
With bowes and arrowes kene,
To ryse the dere out of theyr denne,
Such sightes has ofte bene sene,
As by thre yemen of the north countrey,
By them it is I meane :
The one of them hight Adam Bel,
The other Clym of the Clough,
The thyrd was William of Cloudesly,
An archer good ynough.
They were outlawed for venyson,
These yemen everechone ;
They swore them brethren upon a day,
To Englysshe-wood for to gone.
Now lith and lysten, gentylmen,
That of myrthes loveth to here :
Two of them were singie men,
The third had a wedded fere ;
Wyllyam was the wedded man,
Muche more then was hys care,
He sayde to hys brethren upon a day,
To Caerlel he would fare,
For to speke with fayre Alse hys wife,
And with hys chyldren thre.
By my trouth, sayde Adam Bel,
Not by the counsell of me ;
For if ye go to Caerlel, brother,
And from thys wylde wode wende,
If the justice mai you take,
Your lyfe were at an ende.
If that I come not to morowe, brother,
By pryme to you agayne,
Truste not els but that I am take,
Or else that I am slayne.

He toke hys leaue of his brethren two,
And to Carlel he is gon,
There he knocked at hys owne windowe,
Shortlye and anone.
Where be you, fayre Alyce my wyfe?
And my chyldren three?
Lyghtly let in thyne owne husbande,
Wyllyam of Cloudeslè.
Alas! then sayde fayre Alyce,
And syghed wonderous sore,
Thys place hath ben besette for you,
Thys half yere and more.
Now am I here, sayde Cloudeslè,
I woulde that I in were ;—
Now feche us meate and drynke ynoughe,
And let us make good chere.
She fetched him meat and drynke plenty,
Lyke a true wedded wyfe,
And pleased hym wyth that she had,
Whome she loued as her lyfe.
There lay an old wyfe in that place,
A lytle besyde the fyre,
Whych Wyllyam had found of cherytye
More than seuen yere ;
Up she rose and walked full styll,
Euel mote she spede therefoore,
For she had not set no fote on ground
In seuen yere before.
She went vnto the justice hall,
As fast as she could hye ;
Thys nyght is come vnto this town
Wyllyam of Cloudeslè.
Thereof the iustice was full fayne,
And so was the shirife also :

Thou shalt not trauaile hether, dame, for nought,
Thy meed thou shalt haue or thou go.
They gaue to her a ryght good goune,
Of scarlet it was as I heard sayne,
She toke the gyft and home she wente,
And couched her downe agayne.
They rysed the towne of mery Carlel,
In all the hast that they can,
And came thronging to Wyllyames house,
As fast as they myght goue.
Theyr they besette that good yeman,
Round about on euery syde,
Wyllyam hearde great noyse of folkes,
That heyther ward they hyed.
Alyce opened a shot wyndow,
And loked all about,
She was ware of the justice and shirife bothe,
Wyth a full great route.
Alas! treason! cry'd Aleyce,
Euer wo may thou be !
Go into my chambre, my husband, she sayd,
Swete Wyllyam of Cloudeslè.
He toke hys sweard and hys bucler,
Hys bow and hys chyldren thre,
And wente into his strongest chamber,
Where he thought surest to be.
Fayre Alice folowed him as a louer true,
With her pollaxe in her hande ;
He shal be dead that here cometh in
Thys dore whyle I may stand.
Cloudeslè bent a wel good bowe,
That was of trusty tre,
He smot the justise on the brest,
That hys arrowe brest in thre.

God's curse on his hartt, saide William,
Thys day thy cote dyd on,
If it had ben no better then myne,
It had gone nere thy bone.
Yelde the, Cloudeslè, sayd the justise,
And thy bowe and thy arrowes the fro.
Gods curse on hys hart, sayde fair Alce,
That my husband councelleth so.
Set fyre on the house, saide the sherife,
Syth it wyll no better be,
And brenne we therein William, he saide,
Hys wyfe and chyldren thre.
They fyred the house in many a place,
The fyre flew up on hye ;
Alas ! then cryed fayr Alice,
I se we here shall dy.
William openyd hys backe wyndow,
That was in hys chambre on hye,
And wyth schetes let hys wyfe downe,
And hys chyldren thre.
Have here my treasure, sayde William,
My wyfe and my chyldren thre,
For Christes loue do them no harme,
But wreke you all on me.
Wyllyam shot so wonderous well,
Tyll hys arrowes were all ygo,
And the fyre so fast upon him fell,
That hys bowstryng brent in two.
The spercles brent and fell hym on,
Good Wyllyam of Cloudeslè !
But than wax he a wofull man,
And sayde, thys is a cowardes death to me.
Leuer I had, sayde Wyllyam,
With my sworde in the route to renne,

Then here among myne ennemyes wode,
Thus cruelly to bren.
He toke hys sweard and hys buckler,
And among them all he ran,
Where the people were most in prece,
He smote downe many a man.
There myght no man stand hys stroke,
So fersly on them he ran ;
Then they threw wyndowes and dores on him,
And so toke that good yemàn.
There they hym bounde both hand and fote,
And in depe dongeon hym cast ;
Now, Cloudeslè, sayd the hye justice,
Thou shalt be hanged in hast.
One vow shal I make, sayde the sherife,
A payre of new galowes shall I for the make,
And the gates of Caerlel shal be shutte,
There shall no man come in thereat.
Then shall not helpe Clim of the Cloughe,
Nor yet shall Adam Bell,
Though they came with a thousand mo,
Nor all the deuels in hell.
Early in the mornyng the justice uprose,
To the gates first gan he gon,
And commaundede to be shut full cloce
Lightilè everychone.
Then went he to the market place,
As fast as he coulde hye,
A payre of new gallous there did he up set,
Besyde the pyllory.
A lytle boy stod them amonge,
And asked what meaned that gallow tre ;
They sayde, to hange a good yeamàn,
Called Wyllyam of Cloudeslè.

That lytle boy was the towne swyne heard,
And kept fayre Alyce swyne,
Oft he had seene Cloudeslè in the wodde,
And geuen hym there to dyne.
He went out att a creues in the wall,
And lightly to the wood dyd gone ;
There met he with these wight youge men,
Shortly and anone.
Alas ! then sayde that lytle boye,
Ye tary here all to longe ;
Cloudeslè is taken and dampned to death,
All readye for to honge ;
Alas ! then sayde good Adam Bell,
That ever we see thys daye !
He might her with us have dwelled,
So ofte as we dyd him praye !
He myght have taryed in grene foreste,
Under the shadowes sheene,
And have kepte bothe him and us in reaste,
Out of trouble and teene !
Adam bent a ryght good bow,
A great hart sone had he slayne,
Take that, chylde, he sayde to thy dynner,
And bryng me myne arrowe agayne.
Now go we hence, sayed these wight yong men,
Tary we no lenger here ;
We shall hym borowe, by gods grace,
Though we bye it full dere.
To Caerlel went these good yemèn,
On a mery mornyng of Maye.
Here is a fyt of Cloudeslè,
And another is for to saye.

THE SECOND FIT.

AND when they came to mery Caerlell,
In a fayre mornyng tyde,
They founde the gates shut them vntyll,
Round about on euery syde.
Alas! than sayd good Adam Bell,
That euer we were made men!
These gates be shut so wonderous wel,
That we may not come here in.
Then spake him Clym of the Clough,
Wyth a wyle we wyl vs in bryng;
Let vs saye we be messengers,
Streyght come nowe from our king.
Adam said, I haue a letter written wel,
Now let us wysely werke,
We wyl saye we haue the kinges seales,
I holde the portter no clerke.
Then Adam Bell bete on the gate,
With strokes great and stroug,
The porter herde suche noyse therat,
And to the gate he throng.
Who is there nowe, sayde the porter,
That maketh all thys knocking?
We be tow messengers, sayde Clim of the Clough,
Be come ryght from our kyng.
We haue a letter, sayd Adam Bel,
To the justice we must it bryng;
Let vs in, our messag to do,
That we were agayne to our kyng.
Here commeth none in, sayd the porter,
Be hym that dyed vpon a tre,

Tyll a false thefe be hanged,
Called Wyllyam of Cloudeslè.
Then spake the good yeman Clym of the Clough,
And swore by Mary fre,
And if that we stande longe wythout,
Lyke a thefe hanged shalt thou be.
Lo here we haue the kynges seale ;
What! lordeyne, art thou wode?
The porter went it had been so,
And lyghtly dyd of hys hode.
Welcome be my lordes seale, he saide,
For that ye shall come in.
He opened the gate full shortlye,
An euyl openyng for him.
Now are we in, sayde Adam Bell,
Thereof we are full faine,
But Christ knows, that harowed hell,
How we shall com out agayne.
Had we the keys, said Clim of the Clough,
Ryght wel then shoulde we spede ;
Then might we come out wel ynough,
When we se tyme and nede.
They called the porter to counsell,
And wrange hys necke in two,
And caste him in a depe dongeòn,
And toke hys keys him fro.
Now am I porter, sayde Adam Bel,
Se brother the keys haue we here,
The worst porter to merry Caerlel,
That ye had thys hundred yere :
And now wyll we our bowes bend,
Into the towne wyll we go,
For to delyuer our dere brother,
That lyueth in care and wo.

And thereupon they bent theyr bowes,
And loked theyr stringes were round,
The market place in mery Caerlel,
They beset that stound;
And as they loked them besyde,
A paire of new galowes ther thei see,
And the justice with a quest of squyers,
That had judged Cloudeslè there hanged to be:
And Cloudeslè hymselfe lay redy in a carte,
Faste both fote and hand,
And a stronge rop about hys necke,
All readye for to hange.
The justice called to him a ladde,
Cloudeslè's clothes should he haue,
To take the measure of that yeman,
And therafter to make hys graue.
I haue seen as great a mearveile, saide Cloudeslè,
As betwyne thys and pryme,
He that maketh thys graue for me,
Himselfe may lye therin.
Thou speakest proudli, saide the justice,
I shall the hange with my hande:
Full wel herd hys brethren two,
There styll as they dyd stande.
Then Cloudeslè cast hys eyen asyde,
And saw hys to brethren stand,
At a corner of the market place,
With theyr good bows bent in ther hand,
Redy the justice for to chaunce.
I se comfort, sayd Cloudeslè,
Yet hope I well to fare;
If I might haue my handes at wyll,
Ryght lytle wolde I care.
Then spake good Adam Bell,

To Clym of the Clough so free,
Brother, se ye marke the justyce wel,
Lo yonder ye may him see ;
And at the shyrife shote I wyll,
Strongly with arrowe kene,
A better shote in mery Caerlel
Thys seuen yere was not sene.
They lowsed their arrowes both at once,
Of no man had they dread,
The one hyt the justice, the other the sheryfe,
That both theyr sides gan blede.
All men voyded that them stode nye,
When the justice fell downe to the grounde,
And the sherife fell nyghe hym by,
Eyther had his deathes wounde.
All the citezens fast gan flye,
They durst no longer abyde,
They lyghtly then loused Cloudeslè,
Where he with ropes lay tyde.
Wyllyam sterte to an officer of the towne,
Hys axe out of hys hande he wronge,
On eche syde he smote them downe,
Hym thought he taryed all to long.
Wyllyam sayde to hys brethren two,
Thys daye let us lyue and dye,
If euer you haue nede as I haue now,
The same shall you fynde by me.
They shot so well in that tyde,
For theyr stringes were of silke full sure,
That they kept the stretes on euery side !
That batayle dyd longe endure.
They fought together as brethren tru,
Lyke hardy men and bolde,
Many a man to the ground they thrue,

And many a herte made colde.
But when their arrowes were all gon,
Men preced to them full fast,
They drew theyr swordes then anone,
And theyr bowes from them cast.
They went lyghtlye on theyr way,
Wyth swordes and buclers round,
By that it was myd of the day.
They made mani a wound.
There was an out-horne in Caerlel blowen,
And the belles bacward did ryng ;
Many a woman sayd alas !
And many theyr handes dyd wryng.
The mayre of Caerlel forth com was,
And with hym a ful great route,
These yemen dred him full sore,
For of theyr lyues they stode in great doute.
The mayre came armed a full great pace,
With a pollaxe in hys hande,
Many a strong man with him was,
There in that stowre to stande.
The mayre smot at Cloudeslè with his bil,
Hys bucler he brust in two,
Full many a yeman with great euyll,
Alas ! treason ! they cryed for wo.
Kepe we the gates fast they bad,
That these traytours thereout not go.
But al for nought was that they wrought,
For so fast they downe were layde,
Tyll they all thre, that so manfulli fought,
Were gotten without abraide.
Haue here your keys, sayd Adam Bel,
Myne office I here forsake,
Yf you do by my councèll,

U

A new porter do ye make.
He threw theyr keys at theyr heads,
And bad them euell to thryue,
And all that letteth any good yeman
To come and comfort hys wyfe.
Thus be these good yemen gon to the wod,
And lyghtly as lefe on lynde,
They lough and be mery in theyr mode,
Theyr ennemyes were ferre behynd.
When they came to Englyshe-wode,
Under the trusty tre,
They found bowes full good,
And arrowes full great plentye.
So God me help, sayd Adam Bell,
And Clym of the Clough so fre,
I would we were in mery Caerlel,
Before that fayre meyny.
They set them downe and made good chere,
And eate and drynke full well.
Here is a fet of these wyght yong men,
An other I wyll you tell.

THE THIRD FIT.

As they sat in Englyshe-wood,
Under theyr trusty tre,
They thought they herd a woman wepe,
But her they mought not se.
Sore then syghed the fayre Alyce,
And sayde, alas! that euer I sawe thys daye!
For now is my dere husband slayne,
Alas! and wel a way!

Myght I have spoken wyth hys dere brethren,
Or with eyther of them twayne,
To let them know what him befell
My hart were put out of payne!
Cloudeslè walked a lytle besyde,
And loked vnder the grenewood linde,
He was ware of hys wife and chyldren thre,
Full wo in hart and mynde.
Welcome, wife, then sayde Wyllyam,
Under this trusti tre ;
I had wende yesterday, by swete saynt Johu,
Thou shulde me never have se.
Now well is me, she sayde, that ye be here,
My hart is out of wo.
Dame, he sayde, be mery and glad,
And thanke my brethren two.
Hereof to speake, sayd Adam Bell,
I wis it is no bote ;
The meat that we must supp withall
It runneth yet fast on fote.
Then went they down into a launde,
These noble archares all thre,
Eche of them slew a hart of greece,
The best they could there se.
Haue here the best, Alyce my wyfe,
Sayde Wyllyam of Cloudeslè,
By cause ye so bouldly stod by me,
When I was slayne full nye.
Then went they to supper,
Wyth suche meat as they had,
And thanked God of ther fortune,
They were both mery and glad.
And when they had supped well,
Certayne without any leace,

Cloudeslè sayd, we wyll to our kyng,
To get vs a charter of peace ;
Alyce shal be at our soiournyng,
In a nunry here besyde,
My tow sonnes shall wyth her go,
And ther they shall abyde :
Myne eldest son shall go wyth me,
For hym haue I no care,
And he shall you breng worde agayn
How that we do fare.
Thus be these yemen to London gone,
As fast as they might hye,
Tyll they came to the kynges pallace,
Where they would nedes be.
And whan they came to the kynges courte,
Unto the pallace gate,
Of no man wold they aske no leave,
But boldly went in therat ;
They preced prestly into the hall,
Of no man had they dreade,
The porter came after and dyd them call,
And with them began to chyde.
The ussher sayed, yemen, what wold ye haue ?
I pray you tell me ;
You myght thus make offycers shent :
Good syrs, of whence be ye ?
Syr, we be outlawes of the forest,
Certayne without any leace,
And hether we be come to our kyng,
To get vs a charter of peace.
And whan they came before the kyng,
As it was the lawe of the lande,
They kneled downe without lettyng,
And eche helde vp his hand.

They sayed, lord, we beseche the here,
That ye wyll graunt vs grace,
For we haue slaine your fat falow der,
In many a sondry place.
What be your names ? then said our king,
Anone that you tell me.
They sayd Adam Bel, Clim of the Clough,
And Wyllyam of Cloudeslè.
Be ye those theues, then sayd our kyng,
That men haue tolde of to me ?
Here to God I make a vowe,
Ye shal be hanged al thre ;
Ye shal be dead without mercy,
As I am kynge of this lande.
He commanded his officers everichone
Fast on them to lay hand.
There they toke these good yemen,
And arested them al thre.
So may I thryue, sayd Adam Bell,
Thys game lyketh not me.
But, good lorde, we beseche you now,
That you graunt vs grace,
Insomuche as we be to you comen,
Or els that we may fro you passe,
With such weapons as we haue here,
Tyll we be out of your place ;
And yf we lyue this hundreth yere,
We wyll aske you no grace.
Ye speake proudly, sayd the kynge,
Ye shall be hanged all thre.
That were great pitye, then sayd the quene,
If any grace myght be.
My lorde, whan I came fyrst into this lande,
To be your wedded wyfe,

The fyrst bowne that I wold aske,
Ye would graunt it me belyfe ;
And I asked neur none tyll now,
Therefore, good lorde, graunt it me.
Now aske it, madam, sayed the kynge,
And graunted shall it be.
Then, good my lord, I you beseche,
These yemen graunt ye me.
Madame, ye myght have asked a bowne,
That shuld have ben worth them all thre :
Ye might have asked towres and townes,
Parkes and forestes plenty.
None soe pleasaunt to mi pay, she said,
Nor none so lefe to me.
Madame, sith it is your desyre,
Your askyng graunted shal be ;
But I had leuer have geuen you
Good market townes thre.
The quene was a glad woman,
And sayd, lord, gramarcy,
I dare undertake for them,
That true men shal they be.
But, good lord, speke som mery word,
That comfort they may se.
I graunt you grace, then said our king,
Wasshe, felos, and to meate go ye.
They had not setten but a whyle,
Certayne without lesynge,
There came messengers out of the north,
With letters to our kynge :
And whan they came before the kynge
They kneled downe vpon theyr kne,
And sayd, lord, your offycers grete you wel,
Of Caerlel in the north cuntrè.

How fare my justice, sayd the kyng,
And my sherife also?
Syr, they be slayne, without leasynge,
And many an officer mo.
Who hath them slayne? sayd the kyng,
Anone thou tell me.
Adam Bel, and Clime of the Clough,
And Wyllyam of Cloudeslè.
Alas! for rewth! then sayd our kynge,
My hart is wonderous sore,
I had leuer than a thousand pounde,
I had knowne of thys before;
For I have graunted them grace,
And that forthynketh me,
But had I knowne all thys before,
They had been hanged all thre.
The kyng opened the letter anone,
Hymselfe he red it thro,
And founde how these three outlawes had slaine
Thre hundred men and mo;
Fyrst the justice and the sheryfe,
And the mayre of Caerlel towne,
Of all the constables and catchipolles
Alyue were left not one;
The baylyes and the bedyls both,
And the sergeauntes of the law,
And forty fosters of the fe,
These outlawes had yslaw;
And broke his parks, and slaine his dere,
Ouer all they chose the best,
So perelous out lawes as they were,
Walked not by easte nor west.
When the kynge this letter had red,
In hys harte he syghed sore,

Take vp the table anone he bad,
For I may eate no more.
The kyng called hys best archars,
To the buttes wyth hym to go ;
I wyll se these felowes shote, he sayd,
In the north haue wrought this wo.
The kynges bowmen buske them blyue,
And the quenes archers also,
So dyd these thre wyght yemèn,
With them they thought to go.
There twyse or thryse thay shote about,
For to assay theyr hande,
There was no shote these yemen shot,
That any prycke myght them stand.
Then spake Wyllyam of Cloudeslè,
By him that for me dyed,
I hold hym neuer no good archar
That shuteth at buttes so wyde.
Wherat ? then sayd our kyng,
I pray thee tell me.
At such a but, syr, he sayd,
As men vse in my countree.
Wyllyam went into a fyeld,
And his to brethen with him,
There they set vp two hasell roddes,
Twenty score paces betwene.
I hold him an archar, said Cloudeslè,
That yonder wande cleueth in two.
Here is none suche, sayd the kyng,
Nor none that can so do,
I shall assaye, syr, sayd Cloudeslè,
Or that I farther go.
Cloudeslè, with a bearyng arow,
Claue the wand in to.

Thou art the best archer, then said the king,
Forsothe that euer I se.
And yet for your loue, said Wylliam,
I wyll do more maystry :
I haue a sonne is scuen yere olde,
He is to me full deare,
I wyll hym tye to a stake,
All shall se that be here,
And lay an apele upon hys head,
And go syxe score paces hym fro,
And I myselfe, with a brode arow,
Shall cleue the apple in two.
Now haste the, then sayd the kyng,
By hym that dyed on a tre,
But yf thou do not as thou hast sayde,
Hanged shalt thou be.
And thou touche his head or gowne,
In syght that men may se,
By all the sayntes that be in heaven,
I shall hange you all thre.
That I haue promised, said William,
I wyl it neuer forsake,
And there euen before the kynge,
In the earth he droue a stake,
And bound therto his eldest sonne,
And bad hym stande styll therat,
And turned the childes face fro him,
Because he shuld not sterte ;
An apple vpon his head he set,
And then his bow he bent,
Syxe score paces thay were out met,
And thether Cloudeslè went ;
There he drew out a fayr brode arrowe,
Hys bowe was great and longe,

He set that arrowe in his bowe,
That was both styffe and stronge ;
He prayed the people that was there,
That they would styll stande,
For he that shooteth for such a wager,
Behoueth a stedfast hand.
Much people prayed for Cloudeslè,
That hys lyfe saued myght be,
And whan he made him redy to shote,
There was many a weping eye.
Thus Cloudeslè clefte the apple in two,
That many a man myght se ;
Ouer God's forbode, sayde the kinge,
That thou shote at me !*
I geve the xviii. pence a day,
And my bowe shalt thou beare,
And ouer all the north countre,
I make the chyfe rydere.
And I geve the xvii. pence a day, said the quene,
By God and by my fay,
Come feche thy payment when thou wylt,
No man shall say the nay,
Wyllyam, I make the a gentelman,
Of clothyng and of fe,
And thi two brethren yemen of my chambre,
For they are so semely to se ;

* This seems to be the story of William Tell, founder of the liberties of Switzerland, who was condemned by Gessler, the Austrian governor, to shoot an apple from the head of his son, which he did like Cloudeslè, at the distance of one hundred and thirty paces, without touching the child. He soon afterwards shot the governor. This happened in the year 1307. His instrument was a cross-bow, which is still preserved in the armoury at Zurich. Saxo Grammaticus, however, tells a similar story of Toke and Harold, at a much earlier period, p. 184.

Your sonne, for he is tendre of age,
Of my wyne seller shall he be,
And whan he commeth to mannes estate,
Better auaunced shall he be.
And, Wylliam, bring me your wife, said the quene,
Me longeth her sore to se,
She shal be my chefe gentelwoman,
To gouerne my nursery.
The yemen thanketh them full courteously,
And sayde, to some bysshop wyl we wend,
Of all the synnes that we haue done
To be assoyled at his hand.
So forth be gone these good yemen,
As fast as they myght hye,
And after came and dwelled wyth the kynge,
And dyed good men all thre.
Thus endeth the liues of these good yemen,
God send them eternall blysse !
And all that with hande bowe shoteth,
That of heauen may neuer mysse !

ROBIN HOOD AND THE TANNER'S DAUGHTER.

THE following two ballads were transmitted to the Editor of Gutch's edition by Mr. J. Payne Collier, the well-known Shaksperian commentator, with that kindness and liberality which this gentleman always extends to those who apply to him for assistance in the elucidation or extension of literary pursuits. The source from which they are derived is thus explained by Mr. Collier in his "New particulars regarding the works of Shakespeare, in a letter to the Rev. A. Dyce," 8vo. 1836.

The punctuation of these two ballads is that of the MS., as well as the spelling.

As Robinhood sat by a tree,
   He espied a prettie may,
And when she chanced him to see,
   She turned her head away.

O feare me not, thou prettie mayde,
   And doe not flie from mee,
I am the kindest man, he said,
   That ever eye did see.

Then to her he did doffe his cap,
   And to her lowted low,
To meete with thee I hold it good hap,
   If thou wilt not say noe.

Then he put his hand around her waste,
   Soe small, so tight, and trim,
And after sought her lip to taste,
   And she to kissed him.

Robin Hood and the Tanner's Daughter.—P. 300.

Where dost thou dwell, my prettie maide,
  I prithee tell to mee?
I am a tanner's daughter, she said,
  John Hobbes of Barneslee.

And whither goest thou, pretty maide,
  Shall I be thy true love?
If thou art not afeard, she said,
  My true love thou shalt prove.

What should I feare? then he replied,
  I am thy true love now.
I have two brethren, and their pride
  Would scorn such one as thou.

That will we try, quoth Robinhood,
  I was not made their scorne;
Ile shed my blood to doe the good,
  As sure as they were borne.

My brothers are proude and fierce and strong.
  I am, said he, the same,
And if they offer thee to wrong,
  Theyle find Ile play their game.

Thorough the free forrest I can run,
  The king may not controll,
They are but barking tanners sons,
  To me they shall pay toll.

And if not mine be sheepe and kine,
  I have cattle on my land,
On venison eche day I may dine,
  Whiles they have none in hand.

These wordes had Robinhood scarce spoke,
  When they two men did see,
Come riding till their horses smoke:
  My brothers both, cried shee.

Each had a good sword by his side,
　And furiouslie they rode
To where they Robinhood espied,
　That with the maiden stood.

Flee hence, flee hence, away with speede !
　Cried she to Robinhood,
For if thou stay thoult surely bleede,
　I could not see thy blood.

With us, false maiden, come away,
　And leave that outlawe bolde,
Why fledst thou from thy home this day,
　And left thy father olde ?

Robin stept backe but paces five,
　Unto a sturdie tree,
Ile fight whiles I am left alive ;
　Stay, thou sweete maide, with mee.

He stood before, she stoode behinde,
　The brothers two drewe nie ;
Our sister now to us resign,
　Or thou full sure shalt die.

Then cried the maide, my brethren deare,
　With ye Ile freely wend,
But harm not this young forrester,
　Noe ill doth he pretend.

Stand up, sweete maide, I plight my troth,
　Fall thou not on thy knee ;
Ile force thy cruell brothers both,
　To bend the knee to thee.

Stand thou behinde this sturdie oke,
　I soone will quell their pride ;
Thoult see my sword with furie smoke
　And in their hearts blood died.

He set his backe against a tree,
  His foote against a stone ;
The first blow that he gave so free,
  Cleft one man to the bone.

The tanners bold they fought right well,
  And it was one to two ;
But Robin did them both refell,
  All in the damsells viewe.

The red blood ran from Robins brow,
  All downe unto his knee ;
O holde your handes, my brethren now,
  I will goe backe with yee.

Stand backe, stand backe, my pretty maide,
  Stand backe and let me fight ;
By sweete St. James be no afraide,
  But I will it requite.

Then Robin did his sword uplift,
  And let it fall againe ;
The oldest brothers head it cleft,
  Right through unto his braine.

O holde thy hande, bolde forrester,
  Or ill may thee betide :
Slay not my youngest brother here,
  He is my fathers pride.

Away, for I would scorn to owe,
  My life to the, false maide !
The youngest cried, and aim'd a blow
  That lit on Robins head.

Then Robin leand against the tree,
  His life nie gone did seeme ;
His eyes did swim, he could not see
  The maiden starte betweene.

It was not long ere Robinhood
 Could welde his sword so bright ;
Upon his feete he firmly stood,
 And did renew the fight ;
Untill the tanner scarce could heave
 His weapon in the aire ;
But Robin would not him bereave
 Of life, and left him there.

Then to the greenewood did he fly,
 And with him went the maide ;
For him she vowd that she would dye,
 He'd live for her, he said.

ROBIN HOOD AND THE PEDDLERS.

WILL you heare a tale of Robin Hood,
  Will Scarlett, and Little John?
Now listen awhile, it will make you smile,
  As before it hath many a one.

They were archers three, of hie degree,
  As good as ever drewe bowe;
Their arrowes were long and their armes were
      strong,
  As most had cause to knowe.

But one sommers day, as they toke their way
  Through the forrest of greene Sherwood;
To kill the kings deare, you shall presently
      heare
  What befell these archers good.

They were ware on the roade of three peddlers
      with loade,
  For each one had his packe,
Full of all wares for countrie faires,
  Trust up upon his backe.

A good oke staffe, a yard and a halfe,
  Each one had in his hande;
And they were all boune to Nottingham toune,
  As you shall understand.

Yonder 1 see bolde peddlers three,
  Said Robin to Scarlett and John ;
Wele search their packes upon their backes
  Before that they begone.

Holla, good fellowes ! quod Robin Hood,
  Whether is it ye doe goe ;
Now stay and rest, for that is the best,
  Tis well you should doe so.

Noe rest we neede, on our roade we speede,
  Till to Nottingham we get.
Thou tellst a lowde lye, said Robin, for I
  Can see that ye swinke and swet.

The peddlers three crosst over the lee,
  They did not list to fight.
I charge ye tarrie, quod Robin, for marry,
  This is my owne land by right.

This is my mannor and this is my parke,
  I would have ye for to knowe ;
Ye are bolde outlawes, I see by cause
  Ye are so prest to goe.

The peddlers three turned round to see,
  Who it might be they herd ;
Then again went on as they list to be gon,
  And never answered word.

Then tooke Robin Hood an arrow so good,
  Which he did never lacke,
And drewe his bowe, and the swift arrowe
  Went through the last peddlers packe.

For him it was well on the packe it fell,
  Or his life had found an end ;
And it pierct the skin of his backe within,
  Though the packe did stand his friend.

Then downe they flung their packes each one,
 And stayde till Robin came.
Quod Robin, I saide ye had better stayde ;
 Good sooth, ye were to blame.

And who art thou? by S. Crispin, I vowe,
 Ile quickly cracke thy head !
Cried Robin, come on, all three, or one ;
 It is not so soone done as said.

My name, by the roode, is Robin Hood ;
 And this is Scarlett and John ;
It is three to three, ye may plainelie see,
 Soe now, brave fellowes, laye on.

The first peddlers blowe brake Robins bowe,
 That he had in his hand ;
And Scarlett and John, they eche had one
 That they unneath could stand.

Now holde your handes, cride Robin Hood,
 For ye have oken staves ;
But tarie till wee can get but three,
 And a fig for all your braves.

Of the peddlers the first, his name Kit o Thirske,
 Said, we are well content ;
So eche took a stake for his weapon to make
 The peddlers to repent.

Soe to it they fell, and their blowes did ring well
 Uppon the others backes ;
And gave the peddlers cause to wish
 They had not cast their packes.

Yet the peddlers 3 of their blowes were so free,
 That Robin began for to rue ;
And Scarlett, and John, had such loade laide on,
 It made the sunne looke blue.

At last Kits oke caught Robin a stroke,
   That made his head to sound;
He staggerd, and reelde, till he fell on the
     fielde,
   And the trees with him went round.

Now holde your handes, cride Little John,
   And soe said Scarlett eke;
Our maister is slaine, I tell you plaine,
   He never more will speake.

Now, heaven forefend he come to that end,
   Said Kit, I love him well;
But let him learne to be wise in turne,
   And not with poore peddlers mell.

In my packe, God wot, I a balsame have
     got,
   That soone his hurts will heale;
And into Robin Hoods gaping mouth
   He presentlie powrde some deale.

Now fare ye well, tis best not to tell,
   How ye three peddlers met;
Or if that ye doe, prithee tell alsoe,
   How they made ye swinke and swett.

Poor Robin in sound they left on the ground,
   And hied them to Nottingham,
Whilst Scarlett, and John, Robin tended on,
   Till at length his senses came.

No sooner, in haste, did Robin Hood taste
   The balsame he had tane,
Then he gan to spewe, and up he threwe
   The balsame all againe.

And Scarlett, and John, who were looking on
   Their master as he did lie,
Had their faces besmeared, both eies and beard,
   Therewith most piteouslie.*

Thus ended that fray ; soe beware alwaye
   How ye doe challenge foes ;
Looke well aboute they are not to stoute,
   Or you may nave worst of the blowes.

* This nasty incident seems taken from *Don Quixote*.

THE BOLD PEDLAR AND ROBIN HOOD.

The following ballad is contained in the volume of "Ancient Poems, Ballads, and Songs, of the Peasantry of England," contributed by James Henry Dixon, Esq. to the publications of the Percy Society.

In his introductory notice. Mr. Dixon says, "This ballad is of considerable antiquity. and no doubt much older than some of those inserted in the common garlands. It appears to have escaped the notice of Ritson, Percy, and other collectors of Robin Hood ballads. An aged female in Bermondsey, Surrey, from whose oral recitation the editor took down the present version, informed him, that she had often heard her grandmother sing it, and that it was never in print; but he has of late met with several common stall copies."

There chanced to be a pedlar bold,
  A pedlar bold he chanced to be ;
He rolled his pack all on his back,
  And he came tripping o'er the lee.
    Doun, a doun, a doun, a doun.

By chance he met with two troublesome blades,
  Two troublesome blades they chanced to be ;
The one of them was bold Robin Hood,
  And the other was Little John, so free.

Oh ! pedlar, pedlar, what is in thy pack,
  Come speedilie and tell to me ?
I've several suits of the gay green silks,
  And silken bow-strings two or three.

If you have several suits of the gay green silks,
  And silken bow-strings two or three,
Then it's by my body, cries Little John,
  One half your pack shall belong to me.

Oh! nay, oh! nay, says the pedlar bold,
  Oh! nay, oh! nay, that never can be;
For there's never a man from fair Nottingham
  Can take one half my pack from me.

Then the pedlar he pulled off his pack,
  And put it a little below his knee,
Saying, if you do move me one perch from this,
  My pack and all shall gang with thee.

Then Little John he drew his sword;
  The pedlar by his pack did stand;
They fought until they both did sweat,
  Till he cried, pedlar, pray hold your hand.

Then Robin Hood he was standing by,
  And he did laugh most heartilie;
Saying, I could find a man of a smaller scale,
  Could thrash the pedlar and also thee.

Go you try, master, says Little John,
  Go you try, master, most speedilie,
Or by my body, says Little John,
  I am sure this night you will not know me.

Then Robin Hood he drew his sword,
  And the pedlar by his pack did stand,
They fought till the blood in streams did flow,
  Till he cried, pedlar, pray hold your hand!

Pedlar, pedlar, what is thy name?
  Come speedilie and tell to me;
My name! my name I ne'er will tell,
  Till both your names you have told to me.

The one of us is bold Robin Hood,
  And the other Little John so free :
Now, says the pedlar, it lays to my good will,
  Whether my name I chuse to tell to thee.

I am Gamble Gold of the gay green woods,
  And travell'd far beyond the sea ;
For killing a man in my father's land,
  From my country I was forced to flee.

If you are Gamble Gold of the gay green woods,
  And travelled far beyond the sea,
You are my mother's own sister's son ;
  What nearer cousins then can we be ?

They sheathed their swords with friendly words,
  So merrilie they did agree,
They went to a tavern and there they dined,
  And bottles cracked most merrilie.

ROBIN HOOD'S COURTSHIP WITH JACK CADE'S DAUGHTER.

The game of *Robin Hood* was celebrated in the month of May. The populace assembled previous to the celebration of this festival, and chose some respectable member of the corporation to officiate in the character of *Robin Hood*, and another in that of Little John, his squire. Upon the day appointed, which was on a *Sunday* or a *holiday*, the people assembled in a military array, and went to some adjoining field, where, either as actors or spectators, the whole inhabitants of the respective towns were convened.

The following ballad is contained in an 8vo. publication of about sixteen pages, and was kindly lent to the Editor of Gutch's edition by J. Walter K. Eyton, Esq., of Cheltenham. It was purchased by Mr. Thorpe, the bookseller, at Mr. Brockett's sale, and by him sold to Mr. Eyton. Only fifteen copies were printed.

The title-page is as follows :—

Two Ancient Ballads, Robin Hood's courtship with Jack Cade's Daughter, and The Friers Tragedie. Aberdeen : published and sold by William Robertson. (No date.)

"Brume, brume, on ꝫe hill,
Brume on ꝫe hill for me, oh,
Ye blossomis of ꝫe yellow brume
Are pleasan for to ꝫee, oh."*

* This Chorus is common in many Scotch Ballads. "Broom, Broom on Hill," is a poem mentioned by Lane in his *Progress of Queen Elizabeth into Warwickshire*, as forming part of Captain Cox's collection of ballads, so much adored by the black-letter antiquaries of the present day; now better known as the Roxburgh collection of ballads, at length placed on the shelves of the British Museum.

My native hill is dycht with fleuris,
Sae blomand for to view, oh,
With aureat glades of sucred brume,
An nows of heathery blue, oh.
　　　　　Brume, brume, &c.

ȝe medis are brusit by ȝe fays,
Wi guildis and gowands rair, oh,
An ȝe wilde thyme's sweet smelling breath,
Upon ȝair wings ȝai·bair, oh.
　　　　　Brume, brume, &c.

Als in my bower of eglantyne,
Under ȝe lynden tree, oh,
I heir ȝe little burdes sing,
In ȝair quaeint mynstrelsie, oh.
　　　　　Brume, brume, &c.

An see ȝe burne with birran birr,
Between its cleuchis rin, oh,
An after mony lynkis dreich
Gae loup into ȝe lyn, oh.
　　　　　Brume, brume, &c.

ȝe waters of ȝe loch ȝat rest
In undisturbed repose ;
ȝat stilles the noyis of my heart,
And soothis all my wois.
　　　　　Brume, brume, &c.

God wot ȝat troubled wench I am,
And painet grievouslie.
Quhan on my father's deathe I thinke,
Which causit wes by me.
　　　　　Brume, brume, &c.

An must I leave my bonie woodis,
To gang alang wi' ȝee ;
Gae, gae, your waies, ȝe fair younge manne,
It canna, manna be.
                    Brume, brume, &c.

" Town, town for my monie,
    ȝe town it is for me, oh !
    Ye raffan raket of ȝe town,
    Wassail and revelrie, oh ! "

ȝe stately fortellis of ȝe town
So pertlie stande on hie,
And als ȝe gentlis proud demaynes,
ȝat leukis sae hawtandlie.
                    Town, town, &c.

ȝe schippis ȝat sae guidis full,
Bot to ask us for to bie ;
Alswa ȝe tavernis whar ȝe birle,
ȝe red wine plenteouslie.
                    Town, town, &c.

ȝe schippis ȝat sailis on ȝe sea,
Ar fraught fra fremyt lan,
We wrak of costlyk flagaries,
Baith nippertie an gran.
                    Town, town, &c.

ȝe nonnes quha lukis outwardlie,
Yclad wi modestie ;
ȝe freirs als quha pure of soul
Lernis yame vennerie.
                    Town, town, &c.

An ʒairs ʒe hallis of nobil knychts
Quhare lyart mynstrellis plaies,
An singis for yair lordis delyte,
ʒe feychtes of olden daics.
   Town, town, &c.

Als in ʒat hall is ʒe plaeirs too,
Awand yair mysterie,
Or bawdc interlude befoir
ʒe nobil companie.
   Town, town, &c.

An eke the lymmit gleemen, too,
Quhase gympis makis delycht,
Quhan on ʒe ʒearly minnyng daies
He sporttes all ʒe nycht.
   Town, town, &c.

So come along wi' me, my love,
So come along wi' me, oh!
And I will tak ʒou to ʒe town,
Thae joly sichts to ʒe, on!
   Town, town, &c.

Quhal car I for ʒour fortellis,
Your schippis and demayne, sir;
I wad nae gie my bourik shade
For all ʒour walth an gane, sir.
   Brume, brume, &c.

Ane quaff fra out ʒe chrystal burne
Gat pearlis dernelie, sir,
Is better far ʒan a' ʒour wine
ʒat ʒe birle plenteouslie, sir.
   Brume, brume, &c.

ȝe little skiffe upon ȝe loch
More pleasure is to me, sir,
ȝan ȝour outlandis shippis ȝat
Come from ayont ȝe ȝee, sir.
     Brume, brume, &c.

ȝour nonnes an frieris maȝ defoul
Yaimselves, but sal not me, sir,
ȝair sadde defames I doe reggret,
But nevir wus to see, sir.
     Brume, brume, &c.

ȝour mynstrellis quently carpit rymes,
May give delychte to you, sir ;
ȝe throstle is my quirrister,
And singis me anew, sir.
     Brume, brume, &c.

ȝe rural sportis of ȝe swankis,
More pleasan are to vew, sir,
ȝan mysteries of players leude
And eke ȝour gleemen, too, sir.
     Brume, brume, &c.

Gif you luve me as ȝou say,
ȝou wad not leave this shade, sir ;
Bot ȝou wad live my Robin Hood,
And I ȝour Joan Cade, sir.
     Brume, brume, &c.

And I will nevir from ȝe part,
Bot live within this wode, oh !
An since ȝou will be my Joan Cade,
Ise be your Robin Hood, oh !
     Brume, brume, &c.

ROBIN HOOD AND THE OLD MAN.

A FRAGMENT.

This ballad is taken from the second volume of "Popular
Ballads and Songs," published by Mr. Robert Jamieson
in 1806. For this ballad, Mr. Jamieson acknowledges himself indebted to the Rev. Dr. Percy, the nephew of the
Bishop of Dromore, and editor of several editions of his
"Reliques of Ancient Poetry." Dr. Percy also granted to Mr.
Jamieson the perusal of the celebrated folio MS. of ballads,
from which many of those in the Reliques were selected.
Mr. Jamieson also acknowledges himself indebted for others
to the recitation of Mrs. Brown of Falkland, so well known
to the Scotch collectors.

.   .   .   .

In faith, thou shalt have mine,
And 20s. in thy purse,
   To spend at ale and wine.

Though your clothes are of light Lincolne green,
   And mine gray russet, and torne,
Yet it doth not you beseme
   To doe an old man scorne.*

I scorne thee not, old man, says Robin,
   By the faith of my body ;
Doe of thy clothes, thou shalt have mine,
   For it may noe better be.

* By proposing. that is, to make an exchange of clothes,
the bargain being so much to the advantage of the old
man.

But Robin did on the old mans hose,
  The were torne in the wrist,
When I looke on my leggs, said Robin,
  Then for to laugh I list.

But Robin did on the old mans shoes,
  And the were chitt full cleane ;
Now by my faith, says Little John,
  These are good for thornes keene.

But Robin did on the old mans cloake,
  And it was torne in the necke ;
Now by my faith, said William Scarlett,
  Heere should be set a specke.

But Robin did on the old mans hood,
  Itt goggled on his crowne,
When I come into Nottingham, said Robin,
  My hood it will lightly downe.*

But yonder is an outwood, said Robin,
  An outwood all and a shade,✝
And thither I reede you, my merrymen all,
  The ready way to take.

And when you heare my little horne blow,
  Come raking all on a rowte,

    .   .   .   .

     .   .   .   .

    .   .   horne to his mouth
A loud blast cold he blow,
Full three hundred bold yeomen
  Came raking all on a row.

* *i. e.* I shall easily bare my head, in reverence to the
sheriff. &c.
  ✝ It has been suggested, that this ought to be *brake*, and
not *shade*

But Robin cast downe his baggs of bread,
　　Soe did he his staffe with a face,
And in a doublet of red velvett
　　This yeoman stood in his place.

But Robin he lope, and Robin he threw,
　　He lope over stock and stone,
But those that saw Robin Hood run
　　Said he was a liver old man.

But bend your bowes, and stroke your strings,
　　Set the gallow tree oboute.
And Christes curse on his head, said Robin,
　　That spares the sheriff and the sergeant. *

When the sheriffe see gentle Robin wold shoote,
　　He held up both his hands,
Sayes, aske, good Robin, and thou shalt have,
　　Whether it be house or land.

I will neither have house nor land, said Robin,
　　Nor gold, nor none of thy fee,
But I will have those 3 squires,
　　To greene forrest with mee.

Now marry gods forbett, said the sheriffe,
　　That ever that shold be,
Ffor why they be the kings folons
　　They are all condemned to dye.

But grant me my askynge, said Robin,
　　Or by me faith of my body,
Thou shalt be the first man
　　Shall flower this gallow tree.

But I will　．　．　3 squires

　．　　．　　．　　　．　　．　　．

Cetera desunt.
　　* Should not this be "his rowte"?

THE BIRTH OF ROBIN HOOD.

THE following ballad was taken down from the recitation
of Mrs. Brown, and is here given without the alteration of
a single word. However little historical credit may be due
to it, the account which it gives of the origin of the celebrated English outlaw is certainly very characteristic, and
perfectly consistent with his subsequent life and conduct:
insomuch, that it cannot be said of the renowned hero of
Sherwood, as Deïanira says of Hercules,

————" Dissimiles hic vir et ille puer."
JAMIESON.

O WILLIE's large o' limb and lith,
    And come o' high degree ;
And he is gone to Earl Richard
    To serve for meat and fee.

Earl Richard had but ae daughter,
    Fair as a lilly flower ;
And they made up their love-contract
    Like proper paramour.

It fell upon a simmer's nicht,
    Whan the leaves were fair and green,
That Willie met his gay ladie
    Intil the wood alane.

"O narrow is my gown, Willie,
    That wont to be sae wide ;
And gone is a' my fair colour,
    That wont to be my pride.

Y

" But gin my father should get word
  What's past between us twa,
Before that he should eat or drink,
  He'd hang you o'er that wa.

" But ye'le come to my bower, Willie,
  Just as the sun goes down ;
And kep me in your arms twa,
  And latna me fa' down."

O whan the sun was nere gane down,
  He's doen him till her bower ;
And there, by the lee licht o' the moon,
  Her window she lookit o'er.

Intill a robe o' red scarlet
  She lap, fearless o' harm ;
And Willie was large o' lith and limb,
  And keepit her in his arm.

And they've gane to the gude green wood,
  And ere the night was deen,
She's borne to him a bonny young son,
  Amang the leaves sae green.

Whan night was gane, and day was come,
  And the sun began to peep,
Up and raise the Earl Richard
  Out o' his drowsy sleep.

He's ca'd upon his merry young men,
  By ane, by twa, and by three,
" O what's come o' my daughter dear,
  That she's nae come to me ?

" I dreamt a dreary dream last night,
  God grant it come to gude !
I dreamt I saw my daughter dear
  Drown in the saut sea flood.

"But gin my daughter be dead or sick,
  Or yet be stown awa,
I mak a vow, and I'll keep it true,
  I'll hang ye ane and a'!"

They sought her back, they sought her fore,
  They sought her up and down ;
They got her in the gude grene wood,
  Nursing her bonny young son.

He took the bonny boy in his arms,
  And kist him tenderlie ;
Says, "though I would your father hang,
  Your mother's dear to me."

He kist him o'er and o'er again ;
  "My grandson I thee claim ;
And Robin Hood in gude green wood,
  And that shall be your name."

And mony ane sings o' grass, o' grass,
  And mony ane sings o' corn ;
And mony ane sings o' Robin Hood,
  Kens little whare he was born.

It was na in the ha', the ha',
  Nor in the painted bower ;
But it was in the gude green wood,
  Amang the lilly flower.

ROSE THE RED, AND WHITE LILLY.

THE first of the three following ballads is introduced by Sir Walter Scott, in his "Minstrelsy of the Scottish Border."

The second is included in Mr. Peter Buchan's "Ancient Ballads and Songs of the North of Scotland," 2 vols. Edin. 1828.

Mr. Buchan has also a Scotch ballad entitled, "The Birth of Robin Hood."

The third is taken from Mr. G. P. Kinloch's "Ancient Scottish Ballads."

O ROSE the Red, and White Lilly,
   Their mother dear was dead ;
And their father has married an ill woman,
   Wished them twa little guid.

But she had twa as gallant sons
   As ever brake man's bread ;
And the tane o' them lo'ed her, White Lilly,
   And the tother Rose the Red.

O bigged hae they a bigly bour,
   Fast by the roaring strand ;
And there was mair mirth in the ladyes' bour,
   Nor in a' their father's land.

But out and spake their step-mother,
  As she stood a little forebye—
"I hope to live and play the prank,
  Sall gar your loud sang lie."

She's call'd upon her eldest son ;
  "Cum here, my son, to me :
It fears me sair, my bauld Arthur,
  That ye maun sail the sea."

"Gin sae it maun be, my deir mother,
  Your bidding I maun dee ;
But, be never waur to Rose the Red,
  Than ye hae been to me."

She's call'd upon her youngest son ;
  "Cum here, my son, to me :
It fears me sair, my Brown Robin,
  That ye maun sail the sea."

"Gin it fear ye sair, my mother deir,
  Your bidding I sall dee ;
But, be never waur to White Lilly,
  Than ye hae been to me."

"Now haud your tongues, ye foolish boys !
  For small sall be their part :
They ne'er again sall see your face,
  Gin their very hearts suld break."

Sae Bauld Arthur's gane to our king's court,
  His hie chamberlain to be ;
But Brown Robin, he has slain a knight,
  And to grene-woode he did flee.

When Rose the Red, and White Lilly,
  Saw their twa loves were gane,
Sune did they drop the loud loud sang,
  Took up the still mourning.

And out then spake her White Lilly ;
  "My sister, we'll be gane :
Why suld we stay in Barnisdale,
  To mourn our bour within ?"

O cutted hae they their green cloathing,
  A little abune their knee ;
And sae hae they their yellow hair
  A little abune their bree.

And left hae they that bonny bour,
  To cross the raging sea ;
And they hae ta'en to a holy chapel,
  Was christened by Our Ladye.

And they hae changed their twa names,
  Sae far frae ony toun ;
And the tane o' them's hight Sweet Willie,
  And the tother's Rouge the Rounde.

Between the twa a promise is,
  And they hae sworn it to fulfil ;
Whenever the tane blew a bugle-horn,
  The tother suld cum her till.

Sweet Willie's gane to the king's court,
  Her true love for to see ;
And Rouge the Rounde to gude grene-wood,
  Brown Robin's man to be.

O it fell anes, upon a time,
  They putted at the stane ;
And seven foot ayont them a',
  Brown Robin's gar'd it gang.

She lifted the heavy putting-stane,
  And gave a sad "O hon !"
Then out bespake him, Brown Robin,
  "But that's a woman's moan !"

" O kent ye by my rosy lips ?
   Or by my yellow hair ?
Or kent ye by my milk-white breast,
   Ye never yet saw bare ?"

" I kent na by your rosy lips ;
   Nor by your yellow hair ;
But, cum to your bour whaever likes,
   They'll find a ladye there."

" O gin ye come my bour within,
   Through fraud, deceit, or guile,
Wi' this same brand, that's in my hand,
   I vow I will thee kill."

" Yet durst I cum into your bour,
   And ask nae leave," quo' he ;
" And wi' this same brand, that's in my hand,
   Wave danger back on thee."

About the dead hour o' the night,
   The ladye's bour was broken ;
And, about the first hour o' the day,
   The fair knave bairn was gotten.

When days were gane, and months were come,
   The ladye was sad and wan ;
And aye she cried for a bour woman,
   For to wait her upon.

Then up and spake him, Brown Robin,
   " And what needs this ?" quo' he ;
" Or what can woman do for you,
   That canna be done by me ?"

" 'Twas never my mother's fashion," she said,
   " Nor shall it e'er be mine,
That belted knights should e'er remain
   While ladyes dree'd their pain.

"But gin ye take that bugle-horn,
 And wind a blast sae shrill,
I hae a brother in yonder court,
 Will come me quickly till."

"O gin ye hae a brother on earth,
 That ye lo'e mair than me,
Ye may blow the horn yoursell," he says,
 "For a blast I winna gie."

She's ta'en the bugle in her hand,
 And blawn baith loud and shrill;
Sweet William started at the sound,
 And came her quickly till.

O up and starts him, Brown Robin,
 And swore by Our Ladye,
"No man shall come into this bour,
 But first maun fight wi' me."

O they hae fought the wood within,
 Till the sun was going down;
And drops o' blood, frae Rose the Red,
 Came pouring to the ground.

She leant her back against an aik,
 Said, "Robin, let me be:
For it is a ladye, bred and born,
 That has fought this day wi' thee."

O seven foot he started back,
 Cried, "Alas and woe is me!
For I wished never, in all my life,
 A woman's bluid to see:

"And that all for the knightly vow
 I swore to Our Ladye;
But mair for the sake o' ae fair maid,
 Whose name was White Lilly."

Then out and spake her, Rouge the Rounde,
  And leugh right heartilie,
"She has been wi' ye this year and mair,
  Though ye wistna it was she."

Now word has gane through all the land,
  Before a month was gane,
That a forester's page, in gude grene-wood,
 · Had born a bonny son.

The marvel gaed to the king's court,
  And to the king himsell;
"Now, by my fae," the king did say,
  "The like was never heard tell!"

Then out and spake him, Bauld Arthur,
  And laugh'd right loud and hie—
"I trow some may has plaid the lown,
  And fled her ain countrie."

"Bring me my steid!" the king gan say;
  "My bow and arrows keen;
And I'll gae hunt in yonder wood,
  And see what's to be seen."

"Gin it please your grace," quo' Bauld Arthur,
  "My liege, I'll gang you wi',
And see gin I can meet a bonny page,
  That's stray'd awa frae me."

And they hae chased in gude green-wood,
  The buck but and the rae,
Till they drew near Brown Robin's bour,
  About the close o' day.

Then out and spake the king himsell,
  Says, "Arthur, look and see,
Gin you be not your favourite page,
  That leans against yon tree."

O Arthur's ta'en a bugle-horn,
  And blawn a blast sae shrill;
Sweet Willie started to her feet,
  And ran him quickly till.

"O wanted ye your meat, Willie,
  Or wanted ye your fee?
Or gat ye e'er an angry word,
  That ye ran awa frae me?"

"I wanted nought, my master dear,
  To me ye ay was good:
I cam to see my ae brother,
  That wons in this greue-wood."

Then out bespake the king again,—
  "My boy, now tell to me,
Who dwells into yon bigly bour,
  Beneath yon green aik tree?"

"O pardon me," said sweet Willy,
  "My liege, I dare na tell;
And gang na near yon outlaw's bour,
  For fear they suld you kill."

"O haud your tongue, my bonny boy!
  For I winna be said nay;
But I will gang yon bour within,
  Betide me weal or wae."

They have lighted frae their milk-white steids,
  And saftlie entered in;
And there they saw her, White Lilly,
  Nursing her bonny young son.

"Now, by the mass," the king he said,
  "This is a comely sight;
I trow, instead of a forester's man,
  This is a lady bright!"

O out and spake her, Rose the Red,
   And fell low on her knee :—
"O pardon us, my gracious liege,
   And our story I'll tell thee.

"Our father is a wealthy lord,
   Lives into Barnisdale ;
But we had a wicked step-mother,
   That wrought us meikle bale.

"Yet had she twa as fu' fair sons,
   As e'er the sun did see ;
And the tane o' them lo'ed my sister deir,
   And the tother said he lo'ed me."

Then out and cried him Bauld Arthur,
   As by the king he stood,—
"Now, by the faith of my body,
   This suld be Rose the Red !"

The king has sent for robes o' green,
   And girdles o' shining gold;
And sae sune have the ladyes busked themselves,
   Sae glorious to behold.

Then in and came him, Brown Robin,
   Frae hunting o' the king's deer,
But when he saw the king himsell,
   He started back for fear.

The king has ta'en Robin by the hand,
   And bade him nothing dread,
But quit for aye the gude grene-wood,
   And come to the court wi' speed.

The king has ta'en White Lilly's son,
   And set him on his knee ;
Says, "Gin ye live to wield a brand,
   My bowman thou sall be."

They have ta'en them to the holy chapelle,
   And there had fair wedding ;
And when they cam to the king's court.
   For joy the bells did ring.

THE WEDDING OF ROBIN HOOD
AND LITTLE JOHN.*

THE king has wedded an ill woman,
   Into some foreign land ;—
His daughters twa, that stood in awe,
   They bravely sat and sang.

Then in be-came their step-mother,
   Sae stately stepping ben ; †
"O gin I live and bruik‡ my lip,
   I'll gar § ye change your tune."

"O we sang ne'er that sang, ladie,
   But we will sing again ;
And ye ne'er boor that son, ladie,
   We wad lay our love on.

But we will cow ‖ our yellow locks,
   A little abune our bree ;¶
And we will on to gude green-wud,
   And serve for meat and fee.

And we will kilt** our gay claithing
   A little below the knee ;
And we will on to gude green-wud,
   Gif Robin Hood we see.

* From Kinloch's "Ancient Scottish Ballads."
† *Ben*, inner apartment.   ‡ *Bruik*, enjoy
§ *Gar*, cause.   ‖ *Cow*, clip.
¶ *Abune our bree*, above our brow.   ** *Kilt*, tuck.

And we will change our ain two names,
    When we get frae the toun,—
The tane we will call Nicholas,
    The tither Roger Roun."

Then they hae cow'd their yellow locks,
    A little abune their bree ;
And they are on to gude green-wud
    To serve for meat and fee.

And they hae kilt their gay claithing,
    A little below their knee,
And they are on to gud green-wud,
    Gif Robin Hood they see.

And they hae chang'd thair ain twa names,
    When they gaed frae the toun ;—
The tane they've called Nicholas,
    The tither Roger Roun.

And they hae staid in gude green-wud,
    ·And never a day thought long,
Till it fell ance upon a day,
    That Roger sang a sang.

" When we were in our father's bouer,
    We sew'd the silken seam ;
But now we walk the gude green-wud,
    And bear anither name.

When we were in our father's ha',
    We wore the beaten gold ;
But now we wear the shield so sharp,
    Alas ! we'll die with cold !"

Then up bespake him Robin Hood,
    As he to them drew near ;
" Instead of boys to carry the bow,
    Twa ladies we've got here."

So they had not been in gud green-wud,
  A twalmonth and a day,
Till Roger Roun was as big wi' bairn
  As onie lady could gae.

" O wae be to my stepmother,
  That garr'd me leave my hame,
For I'm wi' bairn to Robin Hood,
  And near nine months is gane.

" O wha will be my bouer-woman,*
  Na bouer-woman is here!
O wha will be my bouer-woman,
  Whan that sad time draws near?

    .   .   .   .

The tane was wedded to Robin Hood,
  And the tither to Little John ;—
And it was a' owing to their step-mother
  That garr'd them leave their hame.

          * *Bouer-woman*, attendant.

ROBIN HOOD AND THE SCOTCHMAN.

THIS ballad appears in an Irish garland, printed at Mona-
ghan, 1796. It is not worthy of notice, otherwise than as
showing the popularity of Robin Hood in Ireland as well
as in Scotland.

Now bold Robin Hood to the north would go,
　With valour and mickle might ;
With sword by his side, which oft had been try'd
　To fight and recover his right.

The first that he met was a jolly stout Scot,
　His servant he said he would be ;
No, quoth Robin Hood, it cannot be good,
　For thou wilt prove false unto me.

Thou hast not been true to sire or cuz ;
　Nay marry, the Scot he said ;
As true as your heart, I never will part,
　Good master be not afraid.

But e'er I employ you, said bold Robin Hood,
　With you I must have a bout ;
The Scotchman reply'd, let the battle be try'd,
　For I know I will beat you out.

Thus saying, the contest did quickly begin,
　Which lasted two hours and more ;
The blows Sawney gave bold Robin so brave,
　The battle soon made him give o'er.

Have mercy, thou Scotchman, bold Robin
  Hood cry'd,
 Full dearly this boon have I bought ;
We both will agree, and my man you shall be,
 For a stouter I never have fought.

Then Sawny consented with Robin to go,
 To be of his bowmen so gay ;
Thus ended the fight, and with mickle delight
 To Sherwood they hasted away.

IN SHERWOOD LIVDE STOUT
ROBIN HOOD.

THE two following ballads were discovered by E. F. Rimbault, Esq. in his extensive and unique collection of ancient music, songs, ballads, madrigals, &c.

IN Sherwood livde stout Robin Hood,
   An archer great, none greater;
His bow and shafts were sure and good,
   Yet Cupid's were much better.
Robin could shoot at many a hart and misse,
Cupid at first could hit a hart of his.
     Hey jolly Robin, hoe jolly Robin, hey jolly
       Robin Hood,
     Love finds out me, as well as thee, so follow
       me, so follow me to the green-wood.

A noble thiefe was Robin Hoode,
   Wise was he could deceive him;
Yet Marrian, in his bravest mood,
   Could of his heart bereave him!
No greater thief lies hidden under skies
Then beauty closely lodgde in womens eyes.
            Hey jolly Robin, &c.

An out-law was this Robin Hood,
   His life free and unruly;
Yet to faire Marrian bound he stood,
   And loves debt paid her duely.

Whom curbe of strictest law could not hold in,
Love with obeyednes and a winke could winne.
> Hey jolly Robin, &c.

Now wend we home, stout Robin Hood,
  Leave we the woods behind us ;
Love-passions must not be withstood,
  Love every where will find us.
I livde in fielde and downe, and so did he,
I got me to the woods, love follow'd me.
> Hey jolly Robin, &c.

From "A Musicall Dreame, or the fourth booke of Ayres, &c." Composed by Robert Jones. London : imprinted by the assignees of William Barley, 1606. A second edition in 1609.

BY LANDS-DALE HEY HO.

From "Deuteromelia ; or the Second Part of Musicks Melodie, or Melodius Musicke, &c. London: printed for Thomas Adams, 1609." 4to.

By Lands-dale hey ho,
  By mery Lands-dale hey ho,
There dwelt a jolly miller,
  And a very good old man was he,
    hey ho.

He had, he had and a sonne a
  Men called him Renold,
And mickle of his might
  Was he, was he, hey ho.

And from his father a wode a,
  His fortune for to seeke,
From mery Lands-dale
  Wode he, wode he, hey ho.

His father would him seke a,
  And found him fast asleepe :
Among the leaves greene
  Was he, was he, hey ho.

He tooke, he tooke him up a,
  All by the lily-white hand,
And set him on his feet,
  And bade him stand, hey ho.

He gave to him a benbow,
   Made all of a trusty tree,
And arrowes in his hand,
   And bad him let them flee.

And shoote was that, that a did a,
   Some say he shot a mile,
But halfe a mile and more
   Was it, was it, hey ho.

And at the halfe miles end a,
   There stood an armed man ;
The childe he shot him through,
   And through and through, hey ho.

His beard was all on a white a,
   As white as whaleis bone,
His eyes they were as cleare
   As christall stone, hey ho.

And there of him they made a
   Good yeoman Robin Hood,
Scarlet, and Little John,
   And Little John, hey ho.

ROBIN HOOD AND THE DUKE OF LANCASTER.

A ballad, to the tune of *The Abbot of Canterbury.*

Tшs ballad was bound up, with many others, in a folio volume, No. —, in a catalogue published a few years ago by Mr. Thorpe the bookseller. The following is the colophon: "London: printed for J. Jones, at the Royal Exchange, and sold by the booksellers of London and Westminster. 1727. (Price 2d)."

It is not to be supposed that this ballad relates to any transactions in the life of our hero. It is in all probability a satire upon some courtier who had made application to the King for the rangership of one of his forests.

COME listen, my friends, to a story so new,
In the days of King John, in twelve hundred and
     two ;
How the bold little Duke of the fair Lancashire
Came to speak to the king like a brave cavalier.
       Derry down, down, down, derry down

In a trice he was got to the good king's abode,
The horse in a froth, on which the duke rode ;
Tho' the steed had galloped full three miles from
     home,
Not so much at the mouth, as the rider did foam.

The gate it did shake, when he knock'd at the
     door,
As his hands they did tremble with anger full
     sore ;

And a message of haste his words did bespeak,
Till the paint, red before, waxed blue on his
cheek.

Quoth the porter, who is it, that dares be so bold
As to stun the fair gate of our liege's freehold;
Quoth the duke, I am come, some truth to
report,
Oho! quoth the porter,—you're just come to
court.

He tossed up his chin, and a roll did advance,
Of parchment I ween, instead of a lance;
See here is the statute, we made such a strife
for;
Said the porter, it seemeth to me all a cypher.

Then up the high steps the short duke he did
stride;
His stride so gigantic his stature belied;
Quoth he, as a peer, I will free my good liege
From the vermin and ear-wigs his grace that
besiege.

The yeoman cried, stand; quoth the duke, I'm a
peer,
And I bring a good statute of parliament here;
Be the king where he can, I may visit him still,
This was passed in the last of Conqueror WILL.

He found his good grace just a trimming his
beard,
By the hands of a dwarf whom he lately had
rear'd;

The duke was beginning his speech in great
    wrath,
Says the king to the dwarf, this is nothing but
    froth.

My good liege, quoth the duke, you are grossly
    abused,
By knaves far and near, by your grace kindly
    used ;
There's your keeper, so crafty, called bold Robin
    Hood,
Keeps us all but himself, my good liege, in a
    wood.

He riseth ere daybreak to kill your fat deer,
And never calls me to partake of the cheer ;
For shoulders and umbles, and other good fees,
He says, for your use he locks up with his keys.

As I'm learnt in the law, this is ROBBING direct,
As appears by the 1st of King WILL : vii. sect.
Besides what is your's, sir, is our's ; and then,
He's a felon, d'ye see, by the 2d of HEN.

What is worse, he will make Harry Gambol a
    keeper ;
And the plot every day is laid deeper and deeper ;
Should he bring him once in, your court would
    grow thinner,
For instead of a saint, he would turn out a
    sinner.

I entreat you, my liege, have a care what you do,
To man, woman, nor child, he was never yet
    true ;

shou'd you trust him he'd serve you as ill, on my
    life,
As he did his first friends, as he did his first wife.

Quoth our liege, would you have no Robin out—
    is that all ?
I would have, quoth the duke, no *Robbing* at all ;
Why, man ! quoth the king, on my troth you'll
    bereave
All my court of its people except 'tis my SHERIFF.

Besides, who'll succeed him ? because, without
    doubt,
You'd have some one put in sure, as well as put
    out.
Then a smile so obliging the duke did display
And made a low beysance, as if who should say.

Said our liege, I respect your great depth at a
    word,
But to cast up vile sums is beneath such a lord.
As to that, quoth the duke, I learnt it at school,
And can tell more than twenty—you know I'm
    no fool.

Quoth our liege, with a sneer, tho' with face right
    serene,
1 believe 1 by this time guess all that you mean ;
Wou'd you have me hang Robin, and count my
    own pelf ;
Oh ! no, quoth the duke, I'd be ROBBING myself.

REFLECTIONS UPON THE STORY OF ROBIN WHOOD AND HIS MEN.

(From Mr. Peck's MSS.)

THE ARGUMENT.—The author compares Robin Whood's times and his own together ; and shows the difference.
The stanza is four lines.   To the tune of *The Outlawing of Robin Whood.*

FULL fourty years and something more
 Robin Whood lived thus !
Fear'd of the rich ; lov'd of the poor ;
 A matter marvelous !

A thing impossible to us
 His story seems to be.
None dare be now so venturous :
 But times are chang'd we see.

We, who in later days do live
 Of better government,
If need be, have a thousand ways
 Such outlaws to prevent.

In Bob's days men more barb'rous were
 And lived less in awe.
Now (heaven be thanked) people fear
 Much more t' offend the law.

Then let's be thankful for these times
    Of plenty, truth, and peace ;
And leave our great and horrid crimes,
    Lest they cause them to cease.

I know there's many a feigned tale
    Of Robin and his crew.
But chronicles, which seldom fail,
    Report these to be true.

Let none think this, or that, a lie ;
    For, were I put to th' worst,
They may the truth of all descry
    I' th' reign of Dick the first.

If any songster please to try,
    As I direction show,
The main of all this history,
    He'll find it true, I know.

And I shall think my labor well
    Bestow'd, to purpose good ;
When 't shall be said that I did tell
    True tales of Robin Whood.

AN ADVENTURE IN SHERWOOD FOREST.

Selected from Hone's Year Book.

THERE strides a warrior dark and grim
Through Sherwood's sylvan shade,
And a battle-ax is held by him,
And keen is its polished blade ;
And he is cased from top to toe
In panoply of steel,
From his nodding horsehair plume, I trow,
To the spur upon his heel.

He pauses ;—fronting in his path
Forth steps a stalworth man ;
The warrior trembled with very wrath,
And his tawny cheek grew wan.
For the stranger's namo was Robin Hood,
And down he flung his glaive ;
"Thou shalt fight," he cried, "or, by the rood,
I will brand thee an errant knave !"

"And I am a chief from Palestine,
So 'tis but meet and right
That I should cross my steel with thine,
Outlaw !" replied the knight.

They fought, and from the crosier's mail
Soon welled a purple flood ;
Yet his blows they fell as quick as hail,
And every blow drew blood.

"A truce !" cried Robin, "thou shalt wend,
Bold swordsman, home with me,
For never did I hope to find
So brave a knight as thee."
"Then lead the way," the knight he said,
Nor Robin made reply,
Though haughty was the warrior's head,
And flashed his piercing eye.

But blithely blew his silver call,
And, ere the echoes slept,
One hundred archers, stout and tall,
Appeared at right and left :
"These are my body-guard, fair sir,
Should fortune prove unkind,
Or foes invade my haunts ; there are
Full fifty more behind.

Yon coppice forms my leafy bower,
My realm is woman's heart :
Woe light on him who braves my power.
Now tell me whom thou art ?"
"I am King Richard !—bowman stay,—
No bending of the knee,
For I have proved thy brand to day,
Nor doubt thy loyalty."

God rest the soul of Robin Hood,
For a gentle thief was he,
As ever ranged the gay green-wood,
God rest his company.

And if ye chance fair Sherwood through
To bend your weary way,
Patter an Ave for Robin Hood,
And his gallant band, I pray.

———

LE MORTE DE ROBIN HODE.

FROM Hone's Every-day Book, where it appears with the following note :—

"Among an odd collection of MS. songs in my possession, I find the following ; which asserts (though without foundation) that the outlaw was *poisoned* by his *sister* the prioress of Kirklees."

To Kirklees stately priorie,
Came an old time-worn man,
And for food and shelter prayed he ;
Ye chief of a noble clan
He was, who in Barnsdale and merrie Sherwood,
Sported blithely in time agone ;
And albeit full cold crept his sluggish blode,
Yt ye step was firm and ye bearing proud,
Of Robin, ye outlawed one.

And ye prioress gave him a brimming bowle,
And bade him drink deep therein,
"'Twould solace," she said, " his fainting soule,"
And her's was a deadlie sinne.
For, although he called her his sister deare,
And she smiled, when she poured for him
Ye sparkling wine, there was poison there,
And herself had mingled the druggs with care
And she pledged her guest, with a thrill of fear,
Though she touch'd but the goblet's brim.

Fearful and long was his dying groan,
As his spirit to Hades fled ;
And the prioress stood like a rooted stone,
When she saw that the erle was dead.
And her eyes grew glazed, and she uttered a yell
Too horrid for mortal ear,
And laughter rang—*'twas the mirth of hell*—
Through that pile so long and drear.

On the self-same night the murdress died,
But she rotted not alone,
For they laid her carcase side by side
With Robin of Huntingdon.
And they placed a fayre stone on ye mossy bed
Of that brave but erring one ;
And many a pilgrim hath wept when he read
What is written that stone upon.

GLOSSARY.

Air, early.

Alderbest, best of all. This phrase, which occurs in Chaucer, is corrupted in de Worde's Edition to "al ther" and "al theyre," which Copland has changed to "al of the," whence it may be inferred that the expression was become already obsolete, and consequently that the poem is of much greater antiquity than 1520; and yet Shakspeare above half a century after puts the word Alderliefest into the mouth of Queen Margaret.

Anker, hermit, anchorite.

Ar, ere.

Asay, Asayed, essayed, tried, proved.

A sound, in a swoon.

Aunsetters, ancestors.

Avow, Avowe, vow.

Avowe, maintain, verbum juris.

Avowè, founder, patron, protector. See Spelman's Glosary, *v.* Advocatus.

Awayte. Awayte me scathe. Lie in wait to do me harm.

Awayted, lay in wait for.

Awet, wit, know.

Awkwarde, backward. An awkwarde stroke seems to mean an unusual or out-of-the-way stroke, one which the receiver could not foresee, be aware of, or guard against, a sort of left or back-hand stroke.

Ayenst, against.

Angels, pieces of gold coin, value 10*s.*

Baist, Baste, basted, belaboured.

Baith, both.

▲ ▲

Bale, mischief, woe, sorrow, misery.

Banis, bane, destruction.

Bear, moan, lamentation, outcry.

Bedene, immediately.

Bedyng, commanding. "Your bedyng shall be doyn," your order shall be obeyed.

Beforen, before.

Begeck. "Give them a begeck." Play them a trick, make fools of them.

Behote, promised.

Bescro, beshrew.

Bestad. ' Ferre and friend bestad," far from home and without a friend. The passage however seems corrupt.

Bestead, beset, put to it.

Beth, are, be.

Blate, sheepish or foolish, as we should now say.

Blive, shortly, by and by.

Bloschems, blossoms.

Bluter, soiled, bedaubed.

Blyve, fast, quickly, briskly.

Bocking, pouring, flowing.

Bode, bidden, invited.

Bolt, Bolte, Boltes, Boltys. A bolt was an arrow of a particular kind used for shooting at a mark or at birds.

Boote, help.

Booting, from *bout*, a struggle, a trial.

Borde, table.

Borowe, pledge, surety.

Borowhode, suretyship.

Boskyd, busked, prepared, got ready.

Bottys, buts.

Bou, bow.

Bound, betook, went, boldly bound away, briskly scampered off.

Bowe, bough.

Bown, ready.

Bowne ye, prepare ye, get ready.

Boyt, both.

Breyde, started, stepped hastily.

Breyde, start, quick or hasty step.

Broke, brook, enjoy, use, keep.

Bronde, brand, sword.

Bushement, ambush.

Buske. "I will me buske," *i.e.* go, betake myself. "Buske you," address or prepare yourselves, make ready.

Bydene, one after another.

Ballup, belly.

Band-dogs, mastiffs; so called from their being usually tied or chained up at night.

Bearing arrow.

Borrow, pledge, bail.

Bottle, a small vessel of wood or leather in the shape of a cask, in which shepherds and others employed abroad in the fields carry or keep their drink.

Brook, enjoy.

Cankardly, peevishly, with ill temper.

Capull hyde, horse hide.

Carel, carle, old fellow.

Cawarde, awkward, or backward. *See* Awkwarde.

Cerstyn, Christian.

Chaffar, chaffer, merchandise, commodity.

Chepe, better chepe, cheaper; a meilleur marché, F. Gret chepe, very cheap; à tres bon marché.

Chepe, cheapen, buy. *Chepyd,* cheapened, bought.

Cheys, choose.

Chorle, churl, peasant, clown.

Cla'd, scratched.

Clock, cloak.

Clouted, patched.

Cole, cowl or hood.

Come (pronounced com), came.

Commytted, accounted.

Corcsed, travelled, hard ridden.

Cortesscy, courteous.

Cote a pye, upper garment, short cloak. Courtepy, Chaucer.

Coud, knew, understood.

Covent, convent; whence our Covent Garden.

Cowed, could, knew. Cowed of curteysey, understood good manners.

Crack, boast.

Craftely, skilfully, secundum artem.

Crouse, brisk.

Cun, con, owe, give.

Curteyse, courteous.

Cutters, sharking fellows.
Can, did.
Carel, Carril, carl, old fellow.
Chiven. "Go play the chiven," make a loud boast or chivey.
Command, warrant, authority.
Counsel, must be counsel to me, *i.e.* must be kept secret; in allusion to the oath of a grand juror.
Curtall, a corruption of cordelier.

Dear, harm.
Demed, judged.
Derne, privy, secret.
Deyell, devil.
Deythe, dight, dressed.
Donne, dun.
Doyt, doth, do.
Dreyffe, drive.
Dub, shallow, miry pool.
Dung, beaten, overcome.
Durk, dagger.
Dyght, dressed, done.
Dysgrate, disgraced. Hath be disgrate, hath fallen into poverty.
Deft, well-looking, neatly dressed.
Depart, part, separate.
Dree, bye.

Een, eyes.
Eftsones, hereafter, afterward.
Eild, age.
Ender, under.
Ere, before.
Eylde, yield.
Eyr, year.
Elephant. ? Eglantine.
English wood. If Inglewood Forest be here meant, the queen is a little out in her geography: she probably means Sherwood, but neither was that in the page's way to Nottingham, and Barnsdale was still further north. *See* Ancient Popular Poetry, 1791, p. 3.
Fail, but fail, without fail, without doubt.
Failyd, wanted, missed.

Fair, fare, ado.
Farley, fairly, plainly.
Fay, faith.
Fayne, glad.
Fe, fee, wages.
Fcardest, fearfulest, most frightened or afraid.
Feders, feathers.
Fend, to ward off, to shift.
Fende, defend.
Fered, fared, lived.
Ferre, far, ferre dayes, far in the day, grand jour, F.
Fette, fetched.
Fetteled him, made him ready, prepared himself, set about.
Fettled, them fettled, attempted, set about.
Feyffe, five.
Flee, fly.
Flinders, splinters.
Fone, foes.
Forbode, commandment.
Forgone, forego, lose.
Fors, care.
Forsoyt, forsooth, truly.
Foryete, forgotten.
Fostere, forester.
Fothe, foot.
Frae, from.
Frebore, free-born, gentle.
Fynly, goodly.
Fare, live.
Finikin, finical, fine, spruce.

Gae, go.
Gan. Gan they gone, are they gone, did they go.
Gang, Gange, go.
Gate, way. *Gates,* ways, passes, paths, ridings. Gate is a
  common word in the North for way.
Geffe, given.
Ger, gear, stuff, goods, property, effects.
Gereamarsey. See Gramercy.
Glen, valley.
God, good, goods, property.
Godamarsey. See Gramercy.
Godde. See God.

Gorney, journey.

Goy, joy.

Gramarcy.   See Gramercy.

Gramercy, thanks, or many thanks ; grand merci, F.

Grce, satisfaction.

Gret, greeted, saluted.

Gripped, grasped, laid hold of.

Grome, a common man (?)

Gang, go.

Gillore, plenty.

God a mercy, gramercy, thanks ; grand mercie, F.

Graff.   "Oak graff."   Oak branch or sapling (?)

Hail.   All hail.   Wholly, entirely.

Halds, holds, holding places, supports.

Halke, perhaps, haugh, low ground by the side of a river (?)
    See the Glossary to Bp. Douglas's Virgil, *v.* Hawchis.
    Halke, with Chaucer, signifies a corner ; but seems here
    used in opposition to hill.

Halfendell, half.

Hals, neck.

Hambellet, ambleth.

Hansell.   The vender of any wares is said to receive hansel
    of his first customer, but the meaning of the text, "Haffe
    hansel for the mar," is not understood unless it can be
    thought to imply, "Give me hansel," *i.e.* buy of my pots.

Haw, the fruit of the white thorn.

Hawt, aught, anything, something.

Hayt, hath.

Held, kept, preserved.

Hende, gentle, courteous.

Hent, took, caught.

Hepe, hip, the fruit of the wild rose.   So in Gil Morice
    Scotish ballad :—

> " I was once as fow of Gill Morrice,
>   As the hip is o' the Hean."

Her, their.

Het, it.

Het, eat.

Heynd, gentle, courteous.

H yt war howte.

Holde, keep.

Hold, held, retained, of council.
Holy, wholly.
Hos, Hus, us.
Hotys, oats.
Housband, manager.
Housbond, husband, peasant.
How, hilL
Howt, out.
Hyght, vowed, promised.
Hynde, knave.
Hart of Greece, means, perhaps, no more than a fat hart, for the sake of a quibble between Greece and grease.
Highed, Hyed, hastened.
Hight. "What they hight," what they are called
Holy dame, our holy dame. The Virgin Mary (so called), unless for "our holy dame" we should read our hali-dome, which may mean our holiness, honesty, chastity, haligdome, sanctimonia, Lye's Saxon Dictionary.

Ibent, bent.
Ibonde, bound.
Ichaunged, changed.
Idyght, dight, dressed, made ready.
Ifedered, feathered.
Ilke, each.
In fere, together.
Inocked, nocked, notched.
Ipight. Up ipyght. *Pican*, pulling, icking.
Iguyt, acquitted, set at liberty.
Iswore, sworn.
Itake, taken.
I, ay.

Japes, tricks.

Kest, cast.
Knave, servant, man.
Kod, quod, quoth, said.
Kyrtell, waistcoat.
Kythe nor kin, acquaintance nor kindred
Kirtle, upper petticoat.

Lappe, wrap.

Late, lake, play, game (?)
Launsgay, a sort of lance.
Leasynge, lying, falsehood.
Leade, train, suite.
Ledesman, guide.
Lese, willing. Whether he were loth or lese, whether he would or not.
Leffe, leave, left.
Leffes, leaves.
Lende, meet, encounter.
Lene, lend.
Lere, learn.
Lere, cheek.
Lese, lose.
Let, omit, hinder, hindered.
Leugh, laughed.
Lever, rather.
Lewte, loyalty, faith, truth; leauté, F.
Leythe, light.
Lithe, attend, hear, hearken.
Losse, love.
Lore, lost.
Lough, Loughe, Low, laughed.
Lowe, "a little hill," P.
Lown, villain, knave, base fellow.
Lust, desire, inclination.
Lyght, light; or perhaps for lyte, little.
Lynde, Lyne, the lime or linden tree; or, collectively, lime trees, or trees in general.
Lyth. See Lithe.
Lyveray, livery, habit, delivery; the mess, portion, or quantity of provisions delivered out at a time by the butler, was called a livery.
Lee, plain.
Ligge, lay.
Lin, stop, stay.

Masars, cups, vessels.
Masterye, "a trial of skill, high proof of skill." P.
Mair, more.
Maney. See Meynè
May, maid.

Me. That ever yet sawe I me. A Gallicism; que jamais j'ai vû moi.

Meal, oatmeal.

Meal-poke, meal bag, bag in which oatmeal is put.

Meat-rife, full of meat or food.

'fede. To quyte hym well his mede, to reward him to some purpose.

Medys, midst, meddle.

Meede, reward.

Met, Mete, measured.

Methe, meat.

Meynè, attendants, retinue; mesnie, F.

Meythe, might.

Mickle, much.

Might, power.

Misters, need, r. mister.

Molde, earth.

Mot, might.

Mote, might, may.

Mote, meeting, assembly, court, audit.

Mountenaunce, amount, duration, space.

Mowe, may.

Muckle. See Mickle.

Myrthes, mirth, merriment. "A man that myrthes can," a minstrel, fiddler, juggler, or the like.

Myster, need.

Main, force.

Mesh. All to mesh, to a mash or jelly.

Mickle, much, great, very.

Mo, more.

Mow, mouth.

Nane, none.

Nar, nor, than.

Ner, ear.

Ner "(ne wer it)," were it not.

Nobellys, nobles. The noble was a gold coin, value 6s. 8d.

Nombles, Numbles, entrails; those parts which are usually baked in a pie: now corruptly called humbles or umbles; nombles, F.

Okerer, usurer.

Os, us.
Owthe, out.
Outdone, undone.

Paid, beat, beaten.
Passe, extent, bounds, limits, district, as the Pas de Calais.
 Copland's edition reads compas.
Pauage, Pavag, Pavage, Pawage, a toll or duty payable for
 the liberty of passing over the soil or territory of an-
 other; paaguim, L.
Pay, content, satisfaction.
Pay, money.
Pecocke. "With Pecocke well y dyght," handsomely
 dressed with peacock feathers. Thus Chaucer, describ-
 ing his "squire's yeman:"

   "A shefe of peacocke arwes bright and kene,
    Under his belt he bare full thriftely."

Plucke, buffet.
Polle, pull.
Poke, bag.
Preke, prick; a piece of wood in the centre of the target.
Prese, company.
Prest, ready, ready to go.
Puding-pricks, skewers that fasten the pudding-bag.
Pyne. "Goddes pyne," Christ's passion or crucifixion.
Palmer. A palmer was properly a pilgrim who had visited
 the holy land, from the palm branch or cross which he
 bore as a sign of such visitation; but, it is probable that
 the distinction between palmers and other pilgrims wa·
 never much attended to in this country. (Mendican
 friars are styled palmers.)
Partaker, assistants, persons to take thy part.
Pinder. The pinder is the pounder or pound keeper; the
 petty officer of a manor, whose duty it is to impound all
 strange cattle straying upon the common, &c.
Quequer, a quick or quickset hedge.
Queyt, quit, recompense.
Quod, quoth, says, said.

Raked, walked apace.
Ray, array, put in order.

Reachles, careless, regardless, unobservant.
Red, clear.
Reuth, pity, compassion.
Reve, take by force.
Reves, bailiffs, receivers.
Ripe, cleansed. *Riped*, cleansed.
Rode, rood, cross.
Rung, staff.
Ruthe, pity, compassion.
Ryall, royal.
Ryalty, royalty.
Ryghtwys, righteous, just.
Ray, battle ray, battle array. The same expression occurs in "The tragicall history of Didaco and Violentia," 1567 :—

> "To traverse forth his grounde, to place
> His troupes in batayle ray."

Rod, poles, perches. A rod, pole, or perch is usually sixteen feet and a half, but in Sherwood Forest (according to Blount) it is twenty-one feet, the foot there being eighteen inches.
Ruth (misprinted truth), pity, compassion.

Sair, sore.
Salved (salued?), saluted.
Scathe, harm.
Schetyng, shooting.
Schomer, summer.
Sclo, slay.
Scoper, supper.
Scouth, scope.
Screje, *Screffe*, sheriff.
Se. *Vide* See.
Seche, seek.
See, regard.
Seker, sure.
Selerer. The cellarer (celerier, cellararius, or cellarius) was that officer who furnished the convent with provisions, cui potus et escæ cura est, qui cellæ vinariæ et escariæ præst. promus (Du Cange). He appears to have been a person of considerable trust, and to have had a principal concern in the management of the Society's revenues See Spelman's Glossary, Fuller's Church History.

Semblaunt, semblance, appearance.
Sete. "Same sete," same state, fashion.
Sette, mortgaged.
Shawe. Shaw is usually explained by little wood; but green wood, little wood, would be mere tautology; it may therefore mean shade, which appears its primitive signification. Scuiva, Saxon.
Shaws, "little woods," P.
Shende, hurt, annoy.
Shente, hurt, wounded.
Shet, shut.
Shete, shoot.
Shope, shaped, made.
Shraddes. See the note.
Shrewde, Shrewed, unlucky.
Shrift, confession.
Shroggs. "Shrubs, thorns, briars, G. Doug. Scroggis."—P.
Shyt, shut.
Skaith, hurt, harm. They feared for its skaith, *i.e.* for the harm it might do them.
Slade. "A slip of greensward between plow-lands or woods, &c."—P.
Slawe, Slone, slain.
Sle, Sloo, slay.
Somers, sumpter-horses.
Sorowe, sorry.
Sothe, sooth, truth.
Sound, See A sound.
Soyt, sooth, truth.
Spear, ask. *Speer'd*, asked, inquired.
Stalward, Stalworthe, stout, well made.
Stane, stone.
Stark, stiff.
Stede, time.
Steven. At some unsett steven, at some unlooked-for time by some odd accident, by mere chance; voice.
Stime, spark, particle or ray of light.
Strang, strong.
Strete, lane, path, way.
Sweaven, dream.
Sweer, stout.
Syne, after, afterward, then.
Syth, afterward.

Sack. A kind of Spanish wine, perhaps sherry, formerly much drunk in this country; very different, at least, from the sweet or Canary wine now so called.

Scop, scalp, pate.

See, regard, protect.

Sets. "Sets with Robin Hood such a lass!" probably such a lass would suit or become him well; but the passage is either singular or corrupt.

Slack, low ground.

Sprunks, pranks, tricks.

Stint, stop.

Sto', store.

Takles, arrows.

Takyll, arrow.

Tene, grief, sorrow, distress, vexation.

Tene, grieve.

The, thrive, prosper.

Thes, thus, this.

Thos, thus.

Throwe, space.

Tortyll, wreathed, twine, twirled, twisted; tortillé, F.

Tray, anger.

Tree, staff.

Treyffe, thrive.

Trow, true.

Trowet, troth.

True, trow, believe.

Trystell, Trystyll.

Tynde, tyndes, tines, antlers, the pointed branches that issue from the main beam of a stag. "In Ynglond ther ys a shepcote, the wyche schepekote hayt ix dorys, and at yeuery dor stondet ix ramys, and every ram hat ix ewys, and yevery ewe hathe ix lambys, and yevery lambe hayt ix hornes, and every horne hayt ix tyndes: what ys the somm of all thes belle?"—(MSS. More, E. 4, 35.)

Twicht, snatched, wrested sharply.

Unketh, uncouth, strange.

Unneth, scarcely.

Up chaunce, by chance.

Venie. Brave venie, merry vein, jovial humour.

Wan. Wonnynge wan, dwelling-place.

Wan, got.

Worse, worse.

Was, wash. " And afterward the justices arise and wasse, and geffe thanks onto the new serjaunts for ther gode dyner."—(Origines juridiciales, p. 115). This ceremony which in former times was constantly practised as well before as after meat seems to have fallen into disuse on the introduction of forks about the year 1620; as before that period our ancesters supplyed the place of this necessary utensil with their fingers.

Wed, Wedde, pawn, pledge, or deposit, to wedde in mortgage, lay my life to wedde, pawn my life.

Welt, welt them at his wyll, did as he pleased with them, used them at his pleasure.

Wend, go.

Wenest, thinkest.

Went, wended, gone.

Werschep, worshipped, reverenced, respected.

West, wist, known.

Wete, know.

Whang, leathern whang, leathern thong or string.

Wight, Wighty, strong. *N.B.* The latter word seems everywhere a mistake for the former.

Wifulle, doubtful.

Win, get.

Wist, knew.

Wode, mad.

Wodys, woods.

Wolwarde, wearing a flannel shirt, by way of penance. *See* Steeven's Shakspeare, 1793, v. 360.

Wonest, dwellest.

Woodweele. " The golden ouzle, a bird of the thrush kind."—P.

Worthe. Wo worthe the, woe be to thee.

Wrack, ruin, destruction.

Wroken, wreaked, revenged.

Wyght, strong, stout.

Wynne, go.

Wis, trow ; there is no modern word precisely synonimous.

Wyte, Wytte, know.

Warden pies. Wardens are a species of large pears. In Shakspeare's "Winter's Tale" the clown, enumerating the articles he had to provide for the sheep-shearing feast, says, '' he must have saffron to colour the warden pies.''

Ware, aware, sensible.

Weele, well.

Wen, wend, go, bye.

Wen. "Marry gep with a wenion."

Whute, whistle.

Wigger wand, wicker wand.

Win. See Wen.

Wist, wis, trou, believe.

Y, I.

Yede, Yeed, went.

Yeff, if.

Yeffell, evil.

Yeft, gift.

Yemenry, yeomanry. "Thow says god yemenry." Thou speakest honestly, fairly, sensibly, like a good yeoman.

Yend, yon.

Yerdes, rods.

Yever, ever.

Yfere, together.

Ylke, same. "Ylke same," very same ; same, very.

Ynowe, enough.

Yode, went.

Yole, Christmass.

Yonder, under.

Yongmen, yeomen (which is everywhere substituted in Copland's edition). See Spelman's Glossary in the words *Juniores, Ycoman;* Tyrwhitt's edition of the "Canterbury Tales," iv. 195. Shakspeare's Plays, 1793, xiv. 347.

Yeomandree, Yeomandry, yeomanry, followers.

www.ingramcontent.com/pod-product-compliance
Lightning Source LLC
Chambersburg PA
CBHW021218270326
41929CB00010B/1180